The Nordic Home

Scandinavian Living, Interiors, and Design

gestalten

The Nordic Home: A Masterclass in Deceptive Simplicity and Stylish Functionality

The continued popularity of architecture and interiors from the Nordic region is a testament to a long evolution of thoughtful design, the desire for simplicity, and a longing for nature reflected in honest, natural materials.

Opposite: Hans J. Wegner's timeless, midcentury designs, including his CH24 Wishbone Chair (1949) and CH337 table (1967), remain mainstays of the Nordic interior. Above: Vega Cottage in a Norwegian Archipelago.

In an increasingly globalized world, it is heartening when buildings, homes, and objects speak of their specific regional identity, reflecting both time and place. While multifaceted and open to many interpretations, the Nordic home is a perfect example of how a region's history, natural landscape, and social conditions can shape its buildings and interiors, even now, when every style of home can be viewed electronically instantly wherever you are.

Nordic design is, above all, functional, and that's a significant reason for its global success. Combine this with high quality and environmental credentials, and Nordic design is a desirable choice for people around the world. The furniture is usually light in form and weight, making pieces easy to fit in and move around. The style is never loud or dominating; it's a design language that doesn't shout, so it's always easy to combine with other styles, including antique furniture. Even the most modern Nordic design works perfectly in historic buildings. For those who think that quality furniture needs to be dipped in gold paint and have cabriole legs, Nordic design is not the solution. The quality is found in the choice of material and the execution of construction, not in the shiny surface.

Although often perceived as simply being *modern* in character when contrasted with other regions and countries, on closer scrutiny, Nordic design can also reveal links to the past, referencing everything from the shapes of Viking ships or old farm buildings to 18th-century chairs or vibrant folk costumes. Yet, at its core, there is a simplicity of form with unbroken curves, straight lines, and honest materials that speaks of modernity, and this is what most people associate with Nordic design. It's a forward-looking architecture and design, even when referencing design details from the past; to live like your grandparents has never been a very attractive prospect for Scandinavians. Still, the Nordic home can throw up unexpected contradictions, be it bright colors, startling contours, or rugged materials. Summarizing the whole region's design identity in just a few words would simplify what is actually a very nuanced variety. This book presents this diversity in all its glorious forms across the Nordic nations at the very top of Europe, taking us from Copenhagen to Oslo and Stockholm to Helsinki. We visit homes in the countryside and the cities, featuring both midcentury and the latest interiors.

What most Nordic design and architecture have in common, both in the present and in the past, is the aim of reduction in the design process. This purposeful stripping away of unnecessary decorative elements to let the essence and function of an object or building excel is something that the Nordic countries share with Asia, although they have developed this ethos entirely independently. It can be traced back to Protestant aesthetics; while the Nordic countries today are more atheist than most, the Lutheran faith once dominated. In contrast to the Catholic church, with its highly ornamental paintings of saints and biblical characters, the Lutherans favored much less sentimental or emotional aesthetics. This simplicity should not be confused with presenting a less sophisticated solution to a design problem because making buildings or objects look unadorned is often more complicated than the opposite. Creating the perfect shadow gap where the floor meets a wall instead of using a skirting board or making seamless joints where a chair leg meets a seat requires a better architect or designer than one who simply covers imprecise solutions with decorative elements that serve no other practical purpose. In the wonderful world of Nordic design, less really is more. This constant reduction comes down to a history of not being

Above: Nordic design draws heavily on natural materials inside and out. Interiors often feature marble surfaces and stoneware, while wood is frequently the material of choice for external surfaces. Opposite: In this Copenhagen apartment, furnishings includes Kaare Klint's Addition leather sofa (1933), Hans J. Wegner's wood and woven paper cord CH25 lounge chair (1950), and a 1970s chrome-and-glass coffee table.

a prosperous part of the world, so efficiency and economy were more important than flair. The Nordic countries were industrialized later than their European neighbors, such as Germany and Britain, and agriculture was the main occupation until the start of the 20th century. It's also a more socially equal society than many other countries and has been so for centuries; in the sparsely populated region, the farmhands and maids ate with the head of the house at the same table. Showing off wealth and belongings is not encouraged, something the Danish-Norwegian author Aksel Sandemose efficiently described in a novel from 1933 when he introduced the fictional *Law of Jante*, where the first commandment is "You're not to think you are anything special." All this forms how buildings and objects are thought of, and it celebrates simplicity and honesty in design.

The awareness of product design and architecture runs deep in the region, woven into the national heritage of each country, with design companies such as Artek (Finland) and Louis Poulsen (Denmark) embedded into the daily life of homes and public spaces. Popular and niche media keep the public regularly informed about old and new designs. Therefore, it is no surprise that modern design classics often appear on Nordic postal stamps. They are instantly recognizable to most people and hold significance as national identifiers, almost as strong as the faces of any current kings or queens. Finland even had architect and designer Alvar Aalto on its 50 Markka banknote until the country adopted the Euro; this modernist architect is still one of the most famous Finns globally, even almost five decades after his passing.

CAPITAL
THE KILN BOOK
MAKING POTTERY

Such a deeply rooted design awareness can make bargain hunting for design at flea markets futile; with so many people knowledgeable of what to look for, the competition can be fierce. There are also many overseas collectors from as far away as Japan to compete with, bidding at auction houses and car trunk sales; collecting Scandinavian design objects is popular across the globe. There are, of course, also many interior design stores, some of them very large, stocking items in current production for those who want to get their hands on the best of what is made today. Still, not all Nordic homes look the same, which a quick look at the homes that estate agents have on offer will confirm, and not all of them are defined by Nordic characteristics. Individual preference, taste, and idiosyncrasies sit comfortably alongside, or in some cases trump, regional specificity.

The success of Scandinavian design on a global scale in recent decades has perhaps unfairly created a reputation of Nordic homes as being filled with blonde wood, plank floors, and self-assembly furniture. It is worth remembering that IKEA, the retail giant responsible for much of this reputation, was founded as a mail-order company in 1943 but only expanded outside its core Nordic region during the 1970s, with its first British and U.S. stores opening during the mid-1980s. When the overseas customers in those countries first encountered the concept of modern Scandinavian design in the immediate postwar era, courtesy of international design fairs and exhibitions, IKEA hadn't even opened its first store in Sweden yet. Instead, as we will discuss later, the international popularity of Nordic design emerged decades earlier.

Trends in furniture come and go more slowly than apparel, but interiors are certainly not immune to fashion trends. The 1970s saw a huge rise in the popularity of pine wood. This conifer tree, with its white-yellow sapwood color, was seen at the time as having a fresh look compared to darker woods such as teak, cherry, and mahogany, which had been popular in the previous decades. Pine was used for furniture, small objects, and whole interiors, such as wall and ceiling cladding. This pine trend suited Swedish and Finnish manufacturers particularly well; anyone traveling through those two countries can verify that the pine forests seem almost endless, making pine a local and affordable timber, available in abundance. Having a pine-clad home bar, a pine dining table, or perhaps even a pine home sauna for a truly Nordic look signaled that you were on trend and part of those who moved with the times. By the late 1980s, though, the pine wood vogue had passed, and it was soon regarded as dated. Interestingly, pine wood interiors during those decades had been so dominant across much of Europe and North America that the Nordics are still associated with pine to this day. Trends nevertheless move in cycles, and what falls out of fashion can make a surprising return a few decades later. Now, a new generation is looking at pine wood again. The blonde wood has been allowed back into Nordic homes, and for many, the pale look of a chunky pine table is as retro-cool as 1960s Brutalist architecture.

When we visit the houses in this book, it will be obvious that these are practical homes made to enjoy living in, entertaining, and increasingly working from, as remote working has made the home office so much more than a few binders in a cupboard. Each country has its own cadre of local design classics, often mixed with the best of Italian and U.S. designs, some Castiglioni and Eames perhaps. Well-designed kitchens, bathrooms, and lights are essential, not just to look good (although that's important, too) but the actual functionality of things. It comes back to nature and daylight; when socializing outdoors is not an option for half of the year due to cold and darkness, how your home looks and works becomes much more of a priority. It also dictates how people socialize; the British have their pubs and the Italians their trattorias, so they don't necessarily have to entertain at home, while Scandinavians often invite people to their homes. There are also other reasons besides chilly weather and limited daylight; the average Nordic home is larger and the average household smaller than in many other countries, so there is more space and fewer family members around if you want to have guests. We welcome you into the Nordic Home!

Opposite: Pine was a material of choice for this contemporary house in Nesodden, Norway. It has a solid timber frame that is visible both inside and out, and the interior walls are lined with pine between the exposed structural beams.

A Danish Architect's Colorful Summer Dream

With smart, eco-friendly solutions and bold color choices for walls and floors, Anette Meldgaard's summer cottage is light, bright, and playful.

Above: Looking toward the house across the garden, Anette Meldgaard and her family are returning to a more natural state. Behind the house are newly planted fruit trees.

SUMMER COTTAGE

ANETTE MELDGAARD

ZEALAND, DENMARK

From the outside, Danish architect Anette Meldgaard's wooden summer cottage looks quite discreet, sitting on its verdant patch of land in the coastal village of Tisvilde, on Denmark's Zealand. Step inside, however, and you'll find bright, voluminous spaces awash with sea blues and greens and delightful pops of color. The house is a clever union of an original 1960s self-build cottage and a new extension that opens the building up, flooding the interior with light via large picture windows and a band of skylights.

A wide hallway directs the eye through a largely open-plan interior toward the lush garden at the rear. Many of the materials used to style the interior are recycled, such as the mismatched terra-cotta floor tiles that come from various sources, including a local church and the Danish company Petersen Tegl. The blue and green colors on the walls are natural paints, their hues inspired by those of the coastal terrain, and polished concrete tiles line the kitchen floor in a mosaic of red, green, and blue.

Opposite and above: The dominant colors are faded sea greens and blues, which work well with the wooden elements and timeworn terra-cotta tiles.

Opposite: Meldgaard and her family used the original cottage for a year before deciding on the best way to extend it to make the most of the natural light.

The Perfect Expression of Nordic Minimalism

Clad in corrugated aluminum, and giving emphasis to the base materiality of its internal structure, this dwelling captures the essence of Nordic design.

Above: A simple change of color marks the transition from one space to the next, from the dining room to the living room.

HOUSE FOR MOTHER
FÖRSTBERG LING
LINKÖPING, SWEDEN

House for Mother was conceived as a dwelling and studio for architect Björn Förstberg's mother, Maria. The house comprises two parallel volumes of the same dimensions, but with different ceiling heights. In the first, a large, open-plan kitchen, dining room, and living room space is minimally furnished with contemporary Scandinavian furniture—much of it wooden—in natural and neutral tones. The plywood-lined walls retain their natural state in the dining room but are painted white in the living room, visually defining spaces without the need for internal partitions. A polished concrete floor runs throughout, rising to create a low bench along the perimeter of the building.

The second volume, also predominantly white in decor, is split-level with bedrooms upstairs and a small studio below. With all-white walls and textiles and a quirky pine nightstand, the bedroom has a soft, light-colored timber floor. Throughout, the spaces are generous and simply decorated, softened here and there with chunky, textured rugs and fleecy throws.

Opposite: The exterior corrugated aluminum cladding changes appearance constantly as it reflects the activity and color of the sky above. This page, right: Rooms are simply furnished with lightweight pieces in natural materials.

The living room (above), dining room, and kitchen are all in the same volume. The gray kitchen (opposite) offers a dramatic contrast to the otherwise light interior.

A House Built Almost Entirely of Wood, Inside and Out

Seemingly simple at first glance, this Danish dwelling draws on clear lines and the repetition of materials to create calm, harmonious spaces.

Above: In the vast dining space, a robust Douglas fir dining table and bench designed and built by Johannes Lauridsen are paired with Børge Mogensen's Folke chairs.

Above: Sunlight floods into the living room. The couple ran solar path simulations to position the windows to make the most of the natural light through the seasons.
Opposite, top: The cabinets in the kitchen are darker than elsewhere, treated with oil that renders a deep glow.

SJÆLLANDS ODDE HOME

LOUISE SKAFTE AND JOHANNES LAURIDSEN

SJÆLLANDS ODDE, DENMARK

The vacation home of designer Louise Skafte and carpenter Johannes Lauridsen lies on Sjællands Odde, a 10-mile-long (15-kilometer-long) peninsula on the northwest coast of Zealand, Denmark. Built by Lauridsen, it is made almost entirely of wood and has large picture windows with panoramic views of wild meadowland, sea, and sky.

Simple in its construction and layout, the house is toned down yet has an understated sophistication, relying on clever architectural solutions that help maximize the space. There is plenty of hidden storage, for example, and built-in sliding doors. The ceilings, floors, and many of the walls are lined with wood—primarily Douglas fir treated with white linseed oil to render the palest of colors. In the kitchen, the cabinetry is also the work of Lauridsen, as is much of the furniture elsewhere—the couple's bed, the dining table, benches, and even the ladder up to a loft space above. A subtle color palette of the lightest natural tones runs throughout, echoing the hues of the surrounding sun-bleached landscape.

The basic idea of "empty space" was key to the styling of the rooms. Both the primary bedroom (above) and the living room (opposite) have an overwhelming sense of calm.

The house is located at the tip of Denmark's Sjællands Odde; the sun-bleached co ors of the surrounding sky, sand, and meadowland were a major inspiration for the couple.

A Norwegian-Style Cabin with a Midcentury Interior

A house of contrasts, this summer retreat has a dark, rugged exterior with a refined, light, bright, stylized interior.

Above: The single-story cabin has a simple floorplan, with a large living / dining room and two bedrooms at one end. Off to one side are the bathroom, kitchen, and a sauna.

SUMMER HIDEAWAY

EMILY AND CHRISTIAN SONESON

DALARÖ, SWEDEN

Nestled on a forested slope, just a short walk from an idyllic sandy beach on Dalarö in the Stockholm archipelago stands Emily and Christian Soneson's summer hideaway. This robust, Norwegian-style log cabin is almost lost among the trees, with its dark, timeworn exterior and vegetation growing on the roof. Inside, however, the timber walls are whitewashed, and Christian, who has a passion for architecture and design, has artfully filled the rooms with handsome, predominantly midcentury furniture in natural materials such as leather, stone, and wood.

A set of classic Jean Prouvé metal-and-plywood side chairs at one end of the living room circle a marble-topped Eero Saarinen Tulip Table. At the other end, a generous tan-colored leather sofa takes a prime position beneath the huge multipaned window. Textiles bring a vaguely "safari" feel to the mix-zebra print cushions and fleecy throws—a theme that continues on the veranda, where a pair of director's chairs point the sitters' gaze toward the lush garden.

Above and opposite: Inside the house, the walls had already been painted by a previous owner, who also installed the large, multipaned window in the main room.

FRANCIS BACON
FRANCIS BACON

Above: The pergola is bathed in sunlight in the afternoon and evening. The teak table and director's chairs are part of the Kryss range from Skargaarden.

Emily and Christian expanded the open spaces around the house. The garden, bathed in sunlight throughout the day, provides an ideal setting for rest and recuperation from city life.

A Vacation Home for a Summer of Blissful Isolation

Rooted deep in rural Denmark, this robust, rustic dwelling features a creative use of concrete and wood to create a bolthole with a protective, cabin-like appeal.

HILL HOUSE

PAX ARCHITECTS

HELGENÆS, DENMARK

This family summerhouse is the creation of Danish PAX Architects and is set within the hilly landscape of Helgenæs, Denmark. The striking interior is dominated by two contrasting materials, wood and concrete, which have been used largely to define the interior spaces. A concrete core runs through the center of the house, offering structural support and containing the more private spaces—bathrooms and bedrooms—and a fireplace. Revolving around this core are the timber-clad living room, kitchen, and dining room. There are no walls, but changes in height or width define these communal spaces.

Much of the furniture is integral, so bookshelves, cupboards, alcoves, and even the sofa are built into the walls. Furniture that is not built-in—benches, internal doors, and the coffee table—is primarily made from wood left over from the construction process. A few midcentury designs are dotted around, including Arne Jacobsen's Ant chairs and a Kaare Klint Safari chair, all layered with warm, shaggy sheepskins in earthy tones.

Opposite: Looking from the dining room, which is predominantly concrete, through to the timber-clad living room with a built-in sofa set beneath a skylight. This page, right: A dedicated studio space serves as a special spot for being creative and has an integrated alcove for relaxing and sleeping.

Opposite: Overlooking the garden from the separate studio space. Above: The use of wood and concrete is well-balanced.

Above: The house is decorated throughout with beautiful, sculptural pieces of driftwood and dried vegetation from the local beach.
Opposite: Looking across the dining area toward the kitchen.

A Simple Wooden House in Rural Norway

Built for a young couple leading a rural existence, House on Pillars came with a basic brief to design a good and sustainable house on a low budget.

Opposite and above: The natural topography of the site creates a series of outdoor spaces and outlooks onto the rock bed and treetops.

HOUSE ON PILLARS

SANDEN + HODNEKVAM ARCHITECTS

NESODDEN, NORWAY

Long and narrow, this Norwegian home was designed by Oslo and Nesodden-based Sanden + Hodnekvam Architects. Standing on rugged terrain, it is raised on wooden pillars to ensure minimal impact on the existing landscape, a lush but rocky forest clearing. It is constructed in such a way that the bedrooms and bathroom sit at the building's core, surrounded by more communal spaces. Sliding doors separate different zones within the house, allowing sight lines down the length of the space when open, but also affording the occupants moments of privacy when desired.

At the center of the house, an open, light-filled space has a glass roof and big windows that overlook the garden and fjord beyond. Constructed primarily from pinewood, the timbers are equally visible inside the house as they are on the exterior and large structural beams remain exposed. The floors are also made from pine, with recycled brick sections in the winter garden and the sunken living room. Furnishings are simple and rustic, on the whole, characteristic of a simple, rural lifestyle.

Sapiens
CAPITAL
THE KILN BOOK
MAKING POTTERY

Opposite and above: Walls and floors are covered in pine, with recycled brick floors in the winter garden and the sunken living room.

The roof is clad with corrugated metal sheets with overhanging eaves. The open space at the center of the house has a glass roof and big windows.

A Green House for a Swedish Island Wilderness

This 21st-century design takes inspiration from Scandinavian Modernism but adds a more playful twist.

Opposite: When choosing a color for the house exterior, the couple initially considered using iron vitriol and then tar. But eventually it seemed obvious that it should be green to match the surrounding nature.

HILMA AF KLINT

Opposite: A family room on the second floor is a popular spot for playing, games reading, and watching TV.
Above: The downstairs lounge serves as a more formal space for entertaining guests.

GREEN HOUSE

CHARLOTTA HALFWORDSON AND CHRISTER JONSSON

ÄLGÖ, SWEDEN

Seeking a location where they could build a house from scratch, Charlotta Halfwordson and Christer Jonsson settled on a plot on the Swedish island of Älgö that was close to woodland and the sea. Then, enlisting the services of Jonsson's architect father, they built the house of their dreams. The forest location was a primary influence when it came to choosing materials—primarily wood—and the color of the house, a deep forest green.

Influenced by Scandinavian interiors of the 1950s and 1960s, the spaces inside are open plan with high ceilings, particularly in the living room, and they have used a palette of dusky pinks, smoky blues, and warm grays. A set designer by trade, Jonsson built some of the furniture himself, much of it wooden, which the couple have paired with midcentury classics that include Hans J. Wegner's iconic Wishbone Chairs. A key feature of the design is the gridlike wooden framework for the windows, which, coupled with the plywood paneling on the ceiling and the slatted banisters on the stairs, takes Scandinavian Modernism into a more playful direction.

Opposite: The bedroom is painted in a pastel-blue color that took several attempts to perfect.
Above: In the pink kitchen, the table, surrounded by Hans J. Wegner's Wishbone Chairs, is from Tônn Furniture.

Opposite: On the ceilings of the dining room, simple moldings cover the joints where the plywood boards meet.
Above: Outside is a generous, sunny, decked area for alfresco dining in the warmer months.

Recapturing a Free-Spirited 1970s Vibe

Vintage pieces, timeless midcentury classics, and a handful of design icons feature in spaces that exude the essence of modern Finnish interior design.

Above: The rich, honeyed tones of the wood-paneled walls and mosaic parquet flooring catch the sunlight. Rasila was keen to maximize on natural light coming into the house.

VILLA EKKULLA

FINNISH DESIGN SHOP

KIMITOÖN, FINLAND

Tasked with renovating Villa Ekkulla, a largely untouched 1970s dwelling in southwest Finland, Maija Rasila of Finnish Design Shop focused above all on preserving the spirit of the place. And where better to start than the original, beautifully patinaed wood-paneled walls and parquet floor in the living room? With these intact, Rasila layered the interior design with colors and furnishings inspired by the 1970s with a contemporary twist.

In the bedrooms, to complement the wood, she painted the walls in green and cream, adding pops of brighter blue and red. In the living / dining areas, a carefully curated selection of furniture sees vintage Finnish designs, such as Alvar Aalto's 1936 Tank armchairs, alongside midcentury classics that include the Eames's wire dining chairs and an asymmetrical pendant lamp by Isamu Noguchi and more contemporary pieces, such as a Jasper Morrison Cork Family stool and a shaggy wool rug from Hay. Among the 1970s icons are Vico Magistretti's Atollo table lamp and a Louis Weisdorf Multi-Lite pendant.

THE TOUCH

Opposite and above: Metal elements—such as the brass pendant lamp and wire chairs in the dining room—and the occasional primary tones balance beautifully with the wood.

A Bold Take on the Scandinavian Palette

This remodeling of an Oslo family home sees light-wood floors and joinery set against more intense shades of the tones associated with Nordic tradition.

From the newly fitted kitchen (opposite), steps lead down to the conservatory, with cream-colored wainscotting, terrazzo flooring, and a plush ocher sofa (above).

Above: An abundance of wood brings balance to the bold palette, with Douglas fir flooring from Dinesen and solid, ash kitchen cabinets matching the exposed ceiling joists.
Opposite: In the dining area, a storage bench runs the entire width of the room topped by forest-green cushions (top); the entrance to the house in the apple garden (bottom).

THE YELLOW HOUSE IN THE APPLE GARDEN

FAMILIEN KVISTAD

OSLO, NORWAY

This 1950s house sits in a large garden filled with fruit trees. Restricted on what they could do with the exterior because the house lies in a conservation area, local design studio Familien Kvistad set about completely remodeling the interior. They removed several internal partitions on the first floor to create an open-plan space with interconnected living and dining areas. Above, a series of small mezzanines replacing the old loft space opened up the home's interior, exposing the roof beams and doubling the ceiling height in the first-floor bedrooms and bathroom.

Then, against a backdrop of light wood—a Douglas fir floor, solid ash kitchen cabinets, and exposed ceiling joists, Familien Kvistad filled the home with color. A bold take on the Scandinavian palette sees sage green walls balanced with pops of ocher, plum, forest green, and indigo, manifesting in small furniture pieces, glossy tiling, soft furnishings, and the art on the wall. At the heart of the home stands a striking fireplace clad in mustard-yellow Kaufmann tiles.

Opposite, top right: The bathroom is more mellow, combining terrazzo plumbing fixtures with calming green tones. Opposite, top and bottom left: The children's rooms are fun spaces to hang out in. In one, storage is built into the box bed; the other has a staircase that doubles as a shelving unit. Above: The tiled stove makes for a striking feature in its own right.

Above, top: In the main living space, a Model 2065 pendant lamp by Gino Sarfatti is suspended above a Noguchi coffee table and Finn Juhl's iconic Chieftain Chair.

A Well-Preserved 1960s Villa Gets a Loving Makeover

With yellow-brick walls in the living room, brown ceramic tiles in the bathroom, and wooden ceilings throughout, this villa remains little changed since it was built over 60 years ago.

Opposite: The living room, with many of the villa's original features largely intact. The glass table and sofa are second-hand finds. In the corner hangs a paper lamp, its wavy lines echoing those of a sculpture by Emma Agersø Bølle in the foreground.

1960s DANISH VILLA

EMMA AGERSØ BØLLE AND NIKOLAJ BØLLE

NÆSBY ON FUNEN, DENMARK

This 1960s Danish villa is currently owned by Emma Agersø Bølle and Nikolaj Bølle, a young Danish couple who could not believe their luck when they stepped into the house for the first time. "It was really well kept, and we wanted the opportunity to add our own touch and otherwise keep as much of the original as possible," says Emma. Although the kitchen was beyond repair and needed a full upgrade, much of the original built-in storage space remained intact, as did a period-typical slatted wall between the entranceway and the kitchen.

The couple repaired and upgraded the existing features, painting walls in colors to complement the villa's warm wooden surfaces. And without breaking the bank, they filled the rooms with period furnishings, including an original Kludestolen armchair designed by Bernt Petersen—an heirloom from Emma's grandfather—and a white Verner Panton chair, the couple's first joint purchase. In addition to such fine vintage finds are several of Emma's own art objects and small items of papier-mâché furniture.

In the dining room hangs a huge artwork by Michael Kaack, a favorite artist of Emma's. An IKEA kitchen has been taken to a new level with custom-built shelving, an aluminum countertop, and natural stone tiles.

QUINZAINE DE L'ÉLÉGANCE 14-31 AOÛT 1943
GENÈVE
2me CONCOURS
HIPPIQUE
NATIONAL 28-29 AOÛT
Steve Jobs

Opposite: A small workstation has been incorporated within a wall of cupboards and open shelves packed with books, trinkets, and art. This page, top right: The bedroom marks a departure from the color scheme of the rest of the house, with walls in a deep forest green.

Where Scandinavian Understatement Meets Italian Flair

In renovating a regular suburban family house on the outskirts of Stockholm, Luca Nichetto fashions a surprising office space for his vibrant designs.

Opposite: The home's vibrant downstairs interior—here, looking from the living room toward the kitchen. Above: The Pink Villa seen from across the garden.

PINK VILLA

NICHETTO STUDIO

STOCKHOLM, SWEDEN

Set in a quiet Stockholm suburb, this 1940s Swedish villa is a live-in studio space for Italian product designer Luca Nichetto. While the exterior remains classic Sweden, with its gable roof, pink-painted timbers, and wooden veranda, the interior is reconfigured to house a series of private and communal workspaces alongside the more conventional rooms of a domestic dwelling—living room, kitchen, bedrooms, and bathrooms.

Decoration focuses primarily on a pared-back, Scandinavian-style palette of light pastel tones and painted wooden floors, providing the perfect backdrop for the studio's bright, colorful fixtures and furnishings. In the entranceway stands a screen of bright yellow ceramic tiles, and a sculptural coral staircase leads to the floor above. The kitchen has a slightly 1950s vibe with its jet-black worktop and baseboards. Nearly all of the furnishings and accessories are designed by Nichetto, including the striking Eanah sofa in electric blue and the yellow La Chance Float coffee table in the living room.

GINORI 1735
GINORI 1735

Opposite and above: Luca Nichetto is not afraid to mix his styles: pieces in the living room have a postmodern "inflated" look to them, while the kitchen is more 1950s in feel.

Opposite and above: Set against walls that match the pink of the house's exterior are brightly colored furnishings with a predominantly contemporary vibe.

A Haven of Tranquility Infused with the Hues of Summer

This summerhouse situated on the north coast of Zealand, Denmark, has a name that translates as "white-free."

Above: Approaching the house, visitors are greeted by a wild garden that is regularly visited by rabbits and deers. The house is enveloped by a concrete terrace.

Above: The color chosen for the kitchen cabinets was inspired by the seagrass that sways on the nearby beach. The large lamp hanging above the kitchen island came from an old factory. Opposite, top: The lounge chair is a design by renowned Danish midcentury designer Børge Mogensen and was originally intended for outdoor use.

HVIDTFRIT
COLD WET & DARK
TISVILDE, DENMARK

Viewed from the outside, this modest summerhouse almost becomes part of the natural landscape, its Siberian larch cladding, oak-framed windows, and sedum roof melding into the trees of the surrounding forest. Stepping inside the house reveals an altogether different vision, however, one that is bathed in a muted palette of primary colors intended to reflect the warm hues of a Danish summer. This was the directive architect Jeppe Utzon received from his client (who also happened to be his mother), a former colorist whose desire for a home "devoid of white" drove the interior styling.

An open-plan, double-height kitchen and dining area serves as the heart of the home, with an adjacent living room made cozy by lowering the ceiling to single height. The dominant colors are the red epoxy floor and turquoise cabinetry set against birch plywood walls and ceilings. The third primary color can be found in the mustard upholstery of the in-built sofa and the sunshine yellow of the living room coffee table beside it.

Opposite: The double height dining space with glass doors that open onto the garden and ceiling height windows that flood the house with natural light. This page: Through the house, to keep the color scheme simple, lamps are finished in black, as are doorframes, the stove, and small pieces of furniture.

A Timeless Combination of White Finishes and Wood

Little changed for decades, the home of legendary Finnish designers Vuokko and Antti Nurmesniemi is a showcase of mid- to late-20th-century Danish design.

Opposite: Being on three levels half a floor apart, with the bottom story partially underground, the sight lines through the house offer intriguing perspectives.
Above: The green sofa was designed by Antti Nurmesniemi for Vilka.

Opposite: The sea-facing facade is punctuated by large windows. Wooden blinds protect the eyes from the bright rays of the sun glistening on the waves just a few feet away.
Above: Vuokko and Antti wanted their house to be as low as possible so it would be camouflaged behind the cliff—surrounded by trees.

VUOKKO AND ANTTI NURMESNIEMI HOUSE

VUOKKO AND ANTTI NURMESNIEMI

HELSINKI, FINLAND

Long and low, the Nurmesniemis' house is built on three almost entirely open-plan levels, each half a floor apart. The living room dominates the top floor, lined with varnished timber floors below a white metal construction on the ceiling. A wall of bookshelves acts as a divider between this room and Antti's studio workspace. The furniture here—a sofa, coffee table, and several display cabinets—are typically low and made from wood.

The floor below sees a reversal of sorts, with honeyed timbers lining the ceiling above a pristine, white-tiled floor. The dining room—its black-topped, tubular-framed table and chairs of Antti's own design—has floor-to-ceiling windows overlooking the sea. The kitchen is just three steps below. The bottom floor of the house includes a sauna, a swimming pool, and a spacious lounge area. Rooms are furnished throughout with Antti's minimalist designs, which include a set of cast-iron kitchen pots, a green-upholstered sofa for Vilka, and a 1980s Armchair 004 in striking black-and-white striped Vuokko fabric.

This page: All of the rooms feature furnishings designed by Antti. Among the best known are his horseshoe-shaped stool and his 001 steel and rattan armchair.

Opposite and above: The home forms an open, unified space, where walls are kept to a minimum and the stories blend into each other. Besides the iconic furniture, artworks, souvenirs, and books add a rich layer to the pared-down decor.

A Modernist Danish Haven in the Heart of Berlin

The floorplan of this single-story Hansaviertel dwelling is defined by the courtyard at its heart—the "room in the green."

Opposite: The living room runs the entire length of the dwelling. At one end, a wall of built-in shelving acoustically insulates the home from the street.

ATRIUM HOUSE

ARNE JACOBSEN

BERLIN, GERMANY

One of four Atrium Houses designed by midcentury Danish architect Arne Jacobsen in the late 1950s, this single-story dwelling is arranged in a U-shape around an inner courtyard—essentially three "wings" that house the bedrooms, kitchen / dining room, and living room.

At the time of construction, Jacobsen insisted that all fixtures and furnishings were of Danish origin. Many were of his own design, including the teak wall units that still bookend the living room. Though much has now been replaced, the interior styling remains true to the original Gesamtkunstwerk aesthetic, with almost all furnishings, from the kitchen units to the living room furniture, sharing the same language in terms of palette and materials. Colors are restricted primarily to black, white, and gray, and materials to steel, glass, polished stone, wood, and leather. The furniture includes several iconic designs such as Le Corbusier's LC5.F sofa, Marcel Breuer's Wassily chair and Laccio side table, a Poul Henningsen pendant lamp, and many more.

Opposite and above, bottom: The compact kitchen with modular cabinetry and a small dining table has large windows overlooking the central courtyard.
Above, top: In the living room, the furniture—rendered in tubular steel, white plastic laminate, and black leather—offers a who's who of modernist classics.

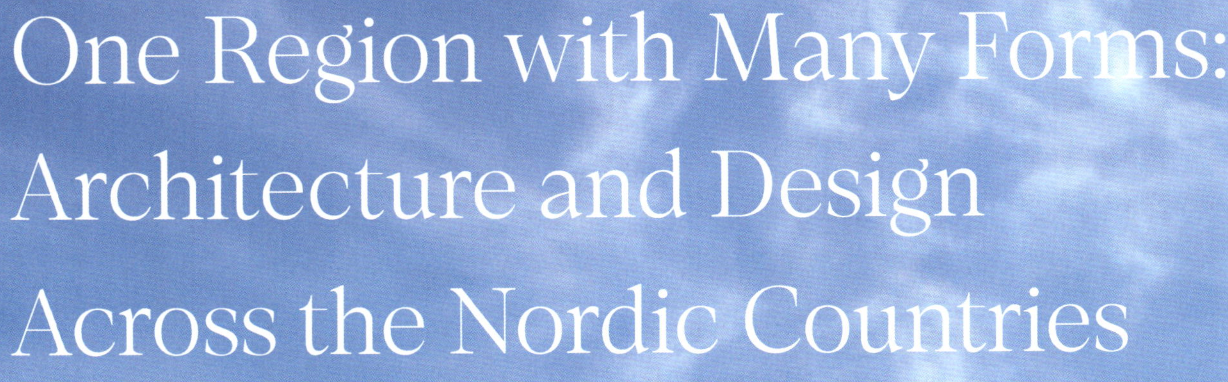

One Region with Many Forms: Architecture and Design Across the Nordic Countries

Far from being homogeneous, the design traditions of the Nordic region are rich in country-specific idiosyncrasies tied to cultural history, weather patterns, and materials found in the local landscape.

Finnish architect Alvar Aalto applied his signature modernist style to a diverse range of buildings, from private residences such as Villa Skeppet in Raseborg, Finland (opposite), to churches such as Santa Maria Assunta in Riola di Vergato, Italy (above).

While often seen by outsiders as having a single cultural identity, the history and landscapes of the Nordic countries have shaped the nations of the region very differently. This has called for alternative design solutions throughout the millennia and still leaves marks today in the built environment and interiors. Denmark, with its flat lowlands, many islands, and agricultural landscape, is very different from Finland, with its abundance of lakes, dense forests, and harsher climate. Outside of the main Danish cities, open fields and farmhouses dominate the landscape, as well as the occasional castle; Denmark had a wealthy nobility who could afford to build grand manor houses and even palaces. This aristocratic class filled their homes with exclusive furniture and objects, which then influenced the wider taste of the nation. Travel to Finland, and there are forests and an almost complete lack of castles, except those designed for defensive purposes because Finland was next to imperial Russia. Most of the nobility lived in Sweden, as the two nations were once one, in the same way that Denmark dominated Norway and Iceland. Norway is divided up by deep and mighty fjords with a long Atlantic coast. Shipping and fishing have long played a key role with ports and ships. Sweden also had a wealthy nobility, and it was more industrialized than its neighbors, which meant that from the 20th century, mass production rather than handicraft shaped the design output of that nation. It also resulted in more urban architecture in the larger Swedish cities, such as Gothenburg. The Second World War impacted the nations and their built environment differently, with Finland and northern Norway seeing major destruction of houses and installations, while Denmark and, in particular, neutral Sweden saw less destruction. The Nordic countries are all less densely populated than many other nations, leaving much unbuilt land, particularly in the northern regions. That gives a closeness to nature, deeply ingrained in the Nordic psyche, and goes a long way to explain why houses and homes are designed to interact with nature rather than escape from it. Nature is seen as something good to be experienced, not as a threat that is best to fence in or escape from.

For those fortunate enough to commission or build their own home or vacation house, there is a great appreciation that quality is worth investing in while still allowing for bold design. Nordic building regulations are generally strict, with inspections following the completion of any building, so it's essential to get the construction right from the start. This attention to detail might increase the project costs, but it also guarantees that homes are safe, long-lasting, and functional. Despite the changes in global temperatures, the Nordic region still has cold winters followed by rainy springs and hot summer days, so houses need to be constructed to function within a wide span of temperatures. This is nothing new, of course; the cold Nordic winter climate has always called for innovative design solutions; pushing moss between timber beams was a common way to improve the insulation of old farmhouses, and carpets and wall hangings were not just for decoration but to stop cold drafts. In the days when most people made their living from the land, it was also important to construct rooms or buildings to store food for the long winters in a region where the growing season is shorter than further south and keep the food safe from rodents and thieves. Luckily, that's not such a problem today. However, energy efficiency is just as important nowadays for environmental reasons and to keep the heating and electricity bills down, so choosing insulation materials and window glazing solutions are always key considerations when building

Both landmark buildings, the city halls of Oslo (above) and Stockholm (opposite) exemplify the use of red brick to create monumental and timeless structures.

new homes. That means finding the most sustainable materials while achieving the best technical results and aesthetics.

When it comes to building styles, there has been a historical dominance of brick architecture in the regions from Denmark to northern Germany, Poland, and the Netherlands, reflecting medieval building traditions. Bricks are, of course, not unique to these countries; Victorian-era London, for example, was dominated by brick buildings, but the classic yellow brick made from London clay looks entirely different from the Gothic red bricks of northern Europe. This dominant use of bricks can also be seen in many buildings in the very south of Sweden, a region that, for a long period, was part of Denmark. Over the centuries, the skill of bricklaying in these countries developed into a fine art, using surface structures, colors, and the orientation of the bricks to decorative effect, and this impacts architecture to the present day. The 20th century saw important Danish brick architecture from architects like Kay Fisker, Peder Vilhelm Jensen-Klint, and Arne Jacobsen, a qualified bricklayer by training. The 21st century has also seen some spectacular brick buildings in Denmark, and it's no surprise that Denmark is the home of LEGO. But it's not just Denmark that has excelled at brick architecture; Alvar Aalto increasingly used brick in his architecture after leaving the white-rendered International Style of the interwar period behind him, most famously in the 1946–48 Baker House Dormitory for MIT in Boston, USA, and the 1950s Muuratsalo experimental house in Jyväskylä, Finland. In Sweden, one of the most famous 20th-century brick buildings is the austere but beautiful 1960s St. Peter's church in the small town of Klippan, in southern Sweden. The renowned architect Sigurd Lewerentz designed it toward the end of his long career and has made Klippan, an otherwise unassuming place, a must-visit site of international architectural pilgrimage. The imposing midcentury Oslo City Hall, as well as the equally impressive City Halls of Stockholm and Copenhagen, all from the 20th century, share a use of somber and heavy red brick to communicate the importance of the building. They are all well worth a visit for both exteriors and interiors.

Once past the flatlands of southern Sweden, the forest belt starts, and with that, the wooden houses. Objects are always shaped by their surroundings and the environment from which they came. Much of the Nordic region is

DJURGARDEN 4

The immersion of buildings in their natural surroundings is a recurring theme. Both Arne Jabcobsen's design for Rødovre town hall (above) and the Snøhetta Viewpoint (opposite) feature walls of glass that bring nature right into the building.

covered with dense forests, so wood has always been the obvious material for houses, interiors, and furniture. Wood from nearby forests is also what kept the furnaces of the many glassworks hot enough to melt sand into glass, so it's also not surprising that it was Finland and Sweden, with their deep forests, which have a particularly strong tradition of glassmaking, with brand names like Iittala, Nuutajärvi, Kosta, and Orrefors represented in design outlets and museums around the world. Each Nordic country has a favorite tree that is closely linked to its furniture production and can be seen in abundance in its interiors. In Finland, it's birch, which is a very light wood that can be seen in shop interiors, airport terminals, and public buildings. In Denmark, it's beech, popular for bentwood chairs, while Sweden uses pine for floors and wall panels, and Norway spruce in much the same way. Oak and ash are also very popular for furniture designs across the region.

Many countries still consider wood an unsuitable building material for houses, based on the fear of fire, which has blighted many cities throughout history. This is not so in the Nordic countries, where wood is used for building construction, and it is increasingly so. Perhaps this is not so surprising when there is living proof that wooden houses can last for a millennium, like the early medieval stave churches in Norway or the old wooden cities like Porvoo in Finland and Eksjö in Sweden. These old wooden houses inspire a modern design that references previous wooden architecture while still being perfectly contemporary. A good example is traditional Falu red paint, often seen on old cottages and barns in Sweden, Finland, and Norway, which is now applied to modern, box-like houses. Building modern private homes out of wood has long been favored by Nordic architects as an alternative to concrete or brick, not least for environmental reasons, and in the last few years, there has also been a surge in interest in constructing larger office buildings and whole blocks of flats made from wood. New techniques have been developed to use compressed, laminated wood to create structural beams as an alternative to steel or concrete. Much research has also gone into the wooden external cladding to make it both fire safety compliant, long-lasting, and pleasing to the eye.

The most common thread uniting new Nordic buildings is the desire to bring nature closer, to blur the border between outside and inside. This is a very different approach to buildings in warmer locations, such as the Mediterranean, when it's important to block the sun's rays and keep rooms as cool as possible, using shutters or louvers. In the Nordic region, windows are large, and doors can often slide to make the outdoor space an extension of the indoor. This can also visually be achieved by continuing the internal material outside; a living room wall can continue uninterrupted onto the terrace. Large panes of glass are often associated with Nordic houses, and for good reason. Even the word "window" is Nordic in origin, from the old Norse *vindauga* or "wind eye," describing an opening in a building where the wind could enter. Thankfully, we now have modern windows that can shield us from the wind and the cold, and Nordic window manufacturers have excelled in producing quality casement and sliding windows. Even in the 19th century, Nordic houses were built with double windows, effectively two sets of window frames, with the 20th century bringing modern double glazing, and from the end of that century, gas-filled double or even triple glazing, now standard. This drive toward large but efficient windows is understandable in the northern hemisphere, where natural daylight is limited to just a few hours each day during the winter. That's also why curtains are often not used much in Nordic homes; they are not needed for insulation, and they block out the much-desired daylight. As window technology has improved, so have the sizes of the windows and sliding doors. This feeds into the Nordic desire to remain close to nature and to bring the outdoors into the home, which is vital to Nordic architects and designers. Scandinavians might appear cool and cosmopolitan, skilfully following the latest trends in fashion, food, and music. Probe them deeper, and it's soon obvious that, at heart, they are rural people who can't wait to return to their summer houses in the archipelago or by a lake in the forest. A large window facing a forest or garden invites nature into the home, filling the inhabitants with an inner calm.

Using local materials is often preferred, and there's been a huge growth in the interest of how traditional building materials and techniques can be used in the 21st century. Paint and lacquers are a good example, also for health reasons as much modern paint and lacquers are chemically made. Cushions or seat covers using Nordic sheepskin covers from free-roaming animals or kitchen countertops or sideboards from local granite are other examples of how local, natural materials can find their way into homes. Recycling material when building houses or interiors also makes good sense, not just for the reduced cost and environmental impact, but because it often brings a visual quality that newly produced material doesn't have.

Good artificial light is much more important when you have less natural light for long periods of the year. The design, shape, and location of electrical lights in the home and workplace are considered very important and worth investing in. It has produced many famous Nordic lighting designers and lighting manufacturers, the most famous perhaps being Poul Henningsen from Denmark, who realized the harm of the naked lightbulb to the eyes and used advanced calculations and models to figure out the optimal light quality. His multi-shade light fittings in glass or metal were also beautiful, making them a staple product in many Nordic homes and beyond. Le Klint's hand-folded white lampshades are another Danish lighting classic that is still very popular. Finland also had a very successful lighting designer in the 20th century, Paavo Tynell, who achieved great export of his designs to the United States, including lights for the Secretary-General of the United Nations. Vintage Tynell lights often now sell for high-figure sums at auctions. In more recent years, plywood lights by the Finnish company Secto have also proven to be an export success.

When brought together, these elements interplay to create what is regarded as the trademarks of modern Nordic design, with wood, nature, and light as the three most important signifiers. Despite endless variations and regional differences, at the core of Nordic design lies a longing for these three elements to seamlessly harmonize into the ideal of a good home.

A Grand Project with a Humble Persona

This elegant, modern design looks to the future while preserving just a little of the past.

Above: Looking toward the house from the pine grove, the kitchen and dining room are visible through the glass.

VILLA BUTTER

ATELJÉ Ö

GOTLAND, SWEDEN

Villa Butter stands on the edge of a 66-foot (20-meter) cliff in Sweden's Gotland, with breathtaking views across the Baltic Sea. The dwelling lies at the heart of a beautiful, ancient pine grove, surrounded by ivy-clad tree trunks and the subtle scent of elderflower in late spring.

Building the house amid the ruins of an earlier structure on the site, the team from Ateljé Ö rendered the exterior in a textured cement to match the roughened surface of an old wall and combined it with oak, glass, and copper to blur the lines between inside and out. With a look that could be described as "modern organic," they then styled the interior to represent "a tamed part of the lushness outside." Spaces are large and open plan, with tiled flooring that continues beyond the facade to form an outdoor terrace. Furniture is predominantly made of wood—finely crafted floor-to-ceiling kitchen cabinets and an elegant, minimal wooden dining table surrounded by Hans J. Wegner's iconic Wishbone Chairs—with soft furnishings and textiles in taupes and tans.

Above: The house lies at the heart of a beautiful, ancient pine grove and offers breathtaking views across the Baltic Sea.

Above and opposite: No matter where you are in the building, the green glow from the ancient pine grove is ever-present as the light catches the foliage.

A Low-Lying Dwelling with a Military History

Almost buried within the landscape, what was once a stony remnant of the past is now a dreamy summer oasis.

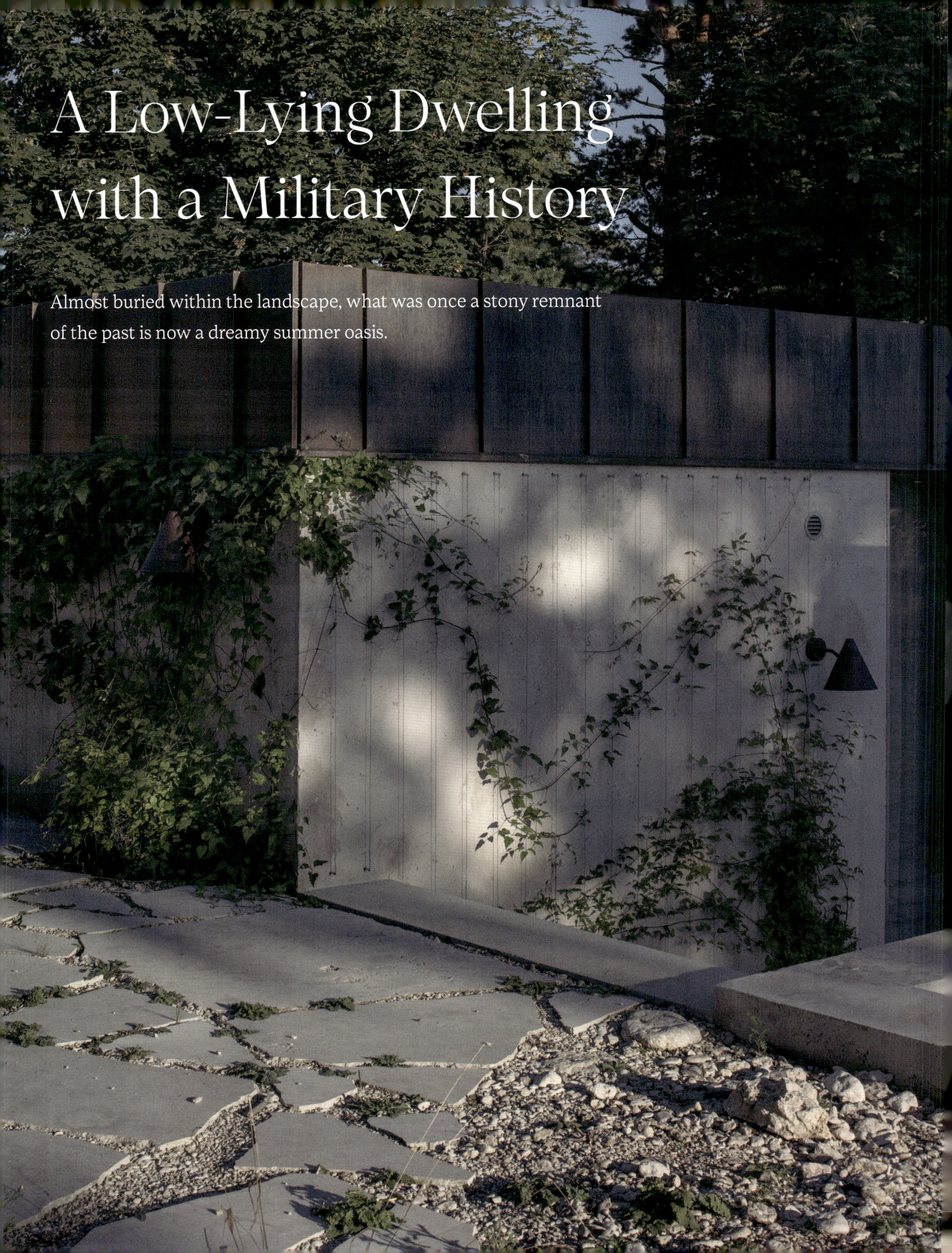

Above: Below a golden, pine-beamed ceiling, the sunken living room features a cor crete floor studded with chunks of local stone.

Opposite: Ateljé Ö created a new, courtyard-type space on the premises, framed by the existing bunker and additional buildings.
Above: Though both are equally earthy, there is a stark contrast between the rough, raw exterior spaces and the more tempered, minimalist interior.

BUNKER 319

ATELJÉ Ö

GOTLAND, SWEDEN

Overlooking the Baltic Sea on the Swedish island of Gotland, this development arose from a partially sunken Cold War bunker. Now comprising a series of low-slung units nestled at the base of a hill, the dwelling retains something of a subterranean vibe, not least because its flat roofs are covered in the site's characteristic gravel. With this, and facades finished in custom rendering and raw wooden pillars, Bunker 319 truly blends in with the low pine trees and muted tones of its surroundings.

The theme continues inside the building, where large chunks of local stone are embedded in the concrete floor—an extension of the landscape's gray hues—and the walls are lined with golden pine. Rooms are simply arranged with wood, cane, and leather furnishings and a palette that echoes the colors of the countryside. Sheer curtains span the floor-to-ceiling windows, blowing gently in the breeze and marking the intersection between new and old, outdoor and indoor, and natural and man-made.

Rather than try to erase the history of the site, the architects embraced the original bunker's form, reinterpreting it for their somewhat brutalist modern-day design.

A Summerhouse Hidden in Hillside Foliage

Barely visible in the height of summer, this graceful, single-story summerhouse seems to float among the treetops, a vision in green.

Above: Perched up among the treetops, inhabitants are totally immersed in nature, constantly surrounded by wildlife and birdsong in the summer months.

Above: The summerhouse has a rectangular floorplan and a custom-designed interior, predominantly in oak. The south-facing facade is almost exclusively made of glass.

SOMMARHOUSE SOLVIKEN

JOHAN SUNDBERG ARKITEKTUR

MÖLLE, SWEDEN

Sheltered from the wind and rain and with generous views out to sea, this elegant summer retreat is resolutely contemporary while blending into its local surroundings. Set in the popular resort of Mölle, on the coast of the Kullaberg peninsula, Sweden, the dwelling is raised on thin steel pillars that truly embed the structure within the landscape.

The house has a simple, rectangular floor plan that places bedrooms, bathrooms, and the laundry toward the rear of the building, while the more public spaces—kitchen and living room—face a wooden terrace and sea views through 30 feet (10 meters) of sliding glass doors. The layout is largely open plan, with one part of the house flowing seamlessly into the next. With a palette that centers on shades of green, the summerhouse is in harmony with its surroundings inside and out. Various elements of the facade—paneling, supporting structure, and railings—have been finished in earthy green tones, while much of the custom-designed interior is made from light oak with green highlights in the soft furnishings.

A Historic Stone House with a Contemporary Twist

Rather than destroy the old to make way for the new, PAX Architects found ways to merge the past with the present.

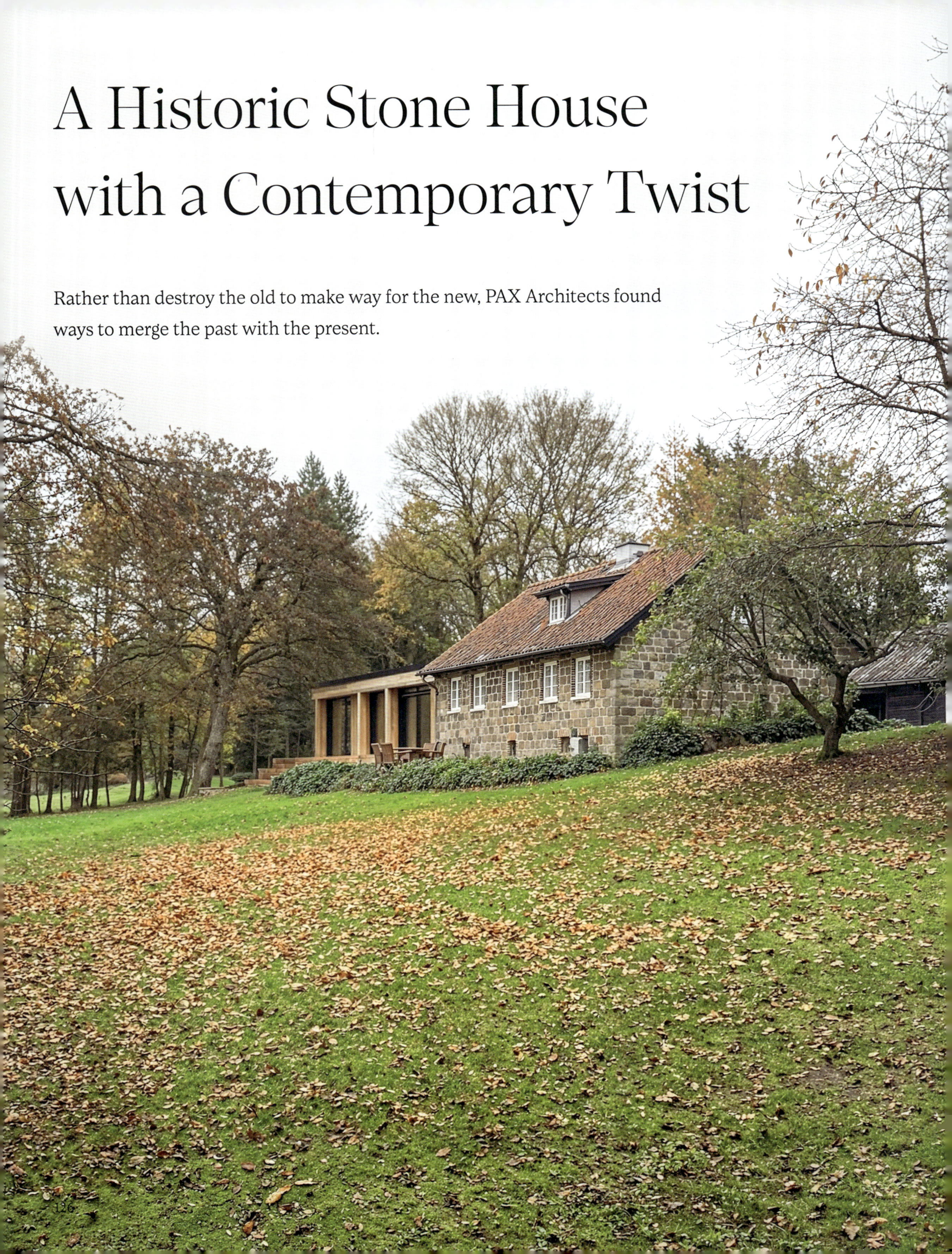

Opposite: Looking across the garden toward the original stone house and its ultramodern timber and glass extension.

BOULDER HOUSE

PAX ARCHITECTS

ØSTBIRK, DENMARK

PAX Architects seamlessly integrate the new with the old in this renovation and extension of a traditional stone house in rural Denmark. It is a project that reflects the desire to respect and preserve local history while finding ways to build homes more sustainably. The extension is unabashedly contemporary—essentially a long, low, timber and glass box, yet what had been the exterior facade of the original house now serves as an interior wall, its rough-hewn boulders taking on a new character and forging a harmonious relationship between past and present.

The new, open-plan living space has generous ceiling heights and expansive windows that offer stunning views across the countryside while flooding the interior with light. Massive, pale-colored timbers line the floor, bringing warmth to the room, furnished with contemporary pieces in neutral tones. The timber continues through a simple aperture in the old stone wall, rising as steps leading into the original house's more intimate, darker spaces.

Opposite: The original, exterior stone walls mark the transition between the dark, low-ceiling kitchen and the higher-ceiling, light-flooded living room.

Capturing the Essence of a Nordic Seascape

A discreet addition to the landscape, this summerhouse is shaped in layers, from the intimacy of the sauna to the ornate living room and kitchen.

Opposite and above: The rear facade of the summerhouse is made of floor-to-ceiling glass partitions that open to the shoreline, just a few feet away from the sea.

Opposite: A deep, timber-lined terrace doubles the living space in summer. Above, right: The view from the sauna at the more private western end of the structure.

SUMMERHOUSE H

JOHAN SUNDBERG ARKITEKTUR

LILLA BEDDINGE, SWEDEN

Located on the southern coast of the Skåne region, this larch-clad summerhouse lies a short distance from the beach and offers views across the Baltic Sea to the south and onto heathland to the east. Essentially a vacation home, the house is a simple box containing a series of volumes with different depths and window treatments. Fully glazed to the south and the east, the rooms progress from the more intimate, private spaces at the western end—the primary bedroom and a sauna—to the more public kitchen, dining, and living rooms, where patio doors open onto a generous, partly covered deck.

Beyond the rough, protective exterior, the rooms are light, bright, and simply furnished. A large, marble-topped island dominates the kitchen, a light-framed sofa faces an open fire in the living room, and Hans J. Wegner Wishbone Chairs flank a solid wood, extendable table in the dining room. A predominantly neutral palette reflects the colors of the Nordic seascape beyond—brilliant-white walls, light-colored timber floors, textiles in a range of grays, and a jute woven rug.

An Ultra-Modern Take on the Swedish Summer House

Dive Architects rise to the challenge of designing a state-of-the art vacation home that has zero impact on the beauty of the natural landscape.

Above: At the meeting point of its two volumes, the house is slightly angled, forming the main entrance and a sheltered outdoor seating area with views across the lake.

DALARNA HOUSE
DIVE ARCHITECTS
BORLÄNGE, SWEDEN

The perfect bolthole, this single-story summerhouse lies three hours north of the Swedish capital, surrounded by a silver birch and pine forest with views overlooking Lake Ösjön. Clad in pine, which will silver beautifully with age, the house, comprising two volumes—one for living, the other for sleeping—is striking for the modernity of its interior.

Whitewashed walls and ceilings rise above a polished concrete slab floor. A rendered brick fireplace and kitchen island is a focal point in the kitchen, living room, and dining area, the only subdivision in the otherwise open-plan space. The wall overlooking the lake is made entirely of glass, so the living spaces are bathed in sunlight from breakfast to late afternoon, and sunsets can be seen from the master bedroom. Every room in the house has access to the decked area outside. Furnishings are timeless and predominantly Scandinavian; they include a Mags Soft Sofa from Hay, Alvar Aalto's brass Golden Bell pendant lamps, and a suite of Arne Jacobsen's dining chairs.

Opposite: A pair of classic French bistro chairs sit on the deck that surrounds the iving room. Above: An Eames rocker adorns the sheltered decking.

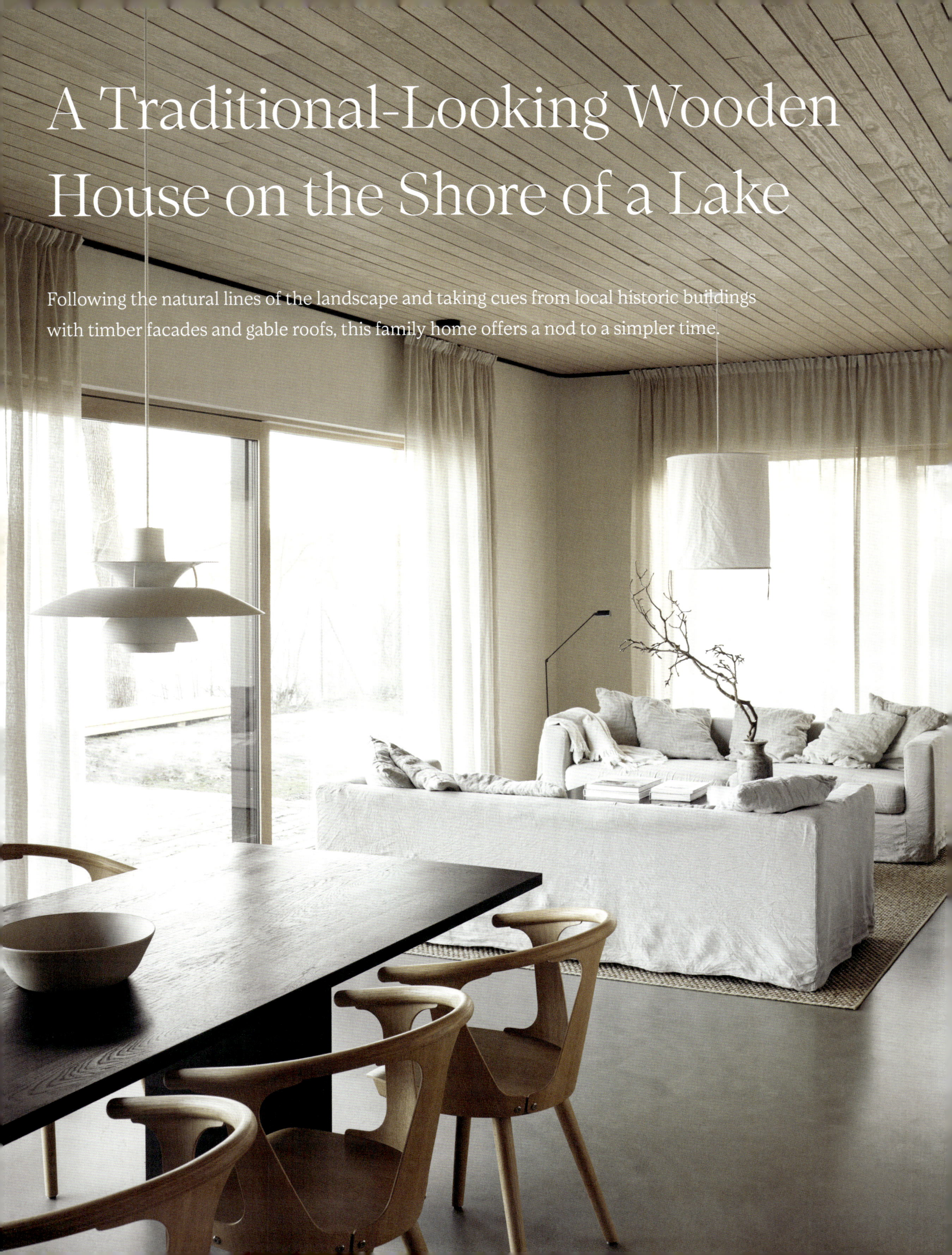

A Traditional-Looking Wooden House on the Shore of a Lake

Following the natural lines of the landscape and taking cues from local historic buildings with timber facades and gable roofs, this family home offers a nod to a simpler time.

Opposite: The open-plan dining room and living room area. All rooms are decorated in the neutral palettes of earthy white, beige, and brown.

VILLA SÖDERGREN

ATELJÉ NORD

SOLLENTUNA, SWEDEN

Gracing the shores of Lake Norrviken in the commuter town of Sollentuna, north of Stockholm, Villa Södergren stands as a modern interpretation of the traditional Swedish barn—essentially, a simple, large-scale building with a pitched roof and wooden facades. In this case, both are made of massive wooden planks treated with black tar to blend in with the natural surroundings.

Inside the house, spaces are orientated to make the most of uninterrupted views toward a nature reserve across the lake. The living room, dining room, and primary bedroom are closest to the water's edge, a few steps down from an open-plan kitchen and the main entrance to the house. In stark contrast to the cool, dark exterior, the interior is soft and warm, light and bright—a polished concrete floor, walls painted in soft chalk colors, and, in keeping with Danish tradition, a ceiling made from knotless pine. Skylights bring natural light into the attic and additional bedrooms on the upper floor.

Opposite: The rooms upstairs are smaller and more compact than the airy spaces below.
Above: A large area of decking leads away from the house and has a built-in, sunken seating area for summer gatherings.

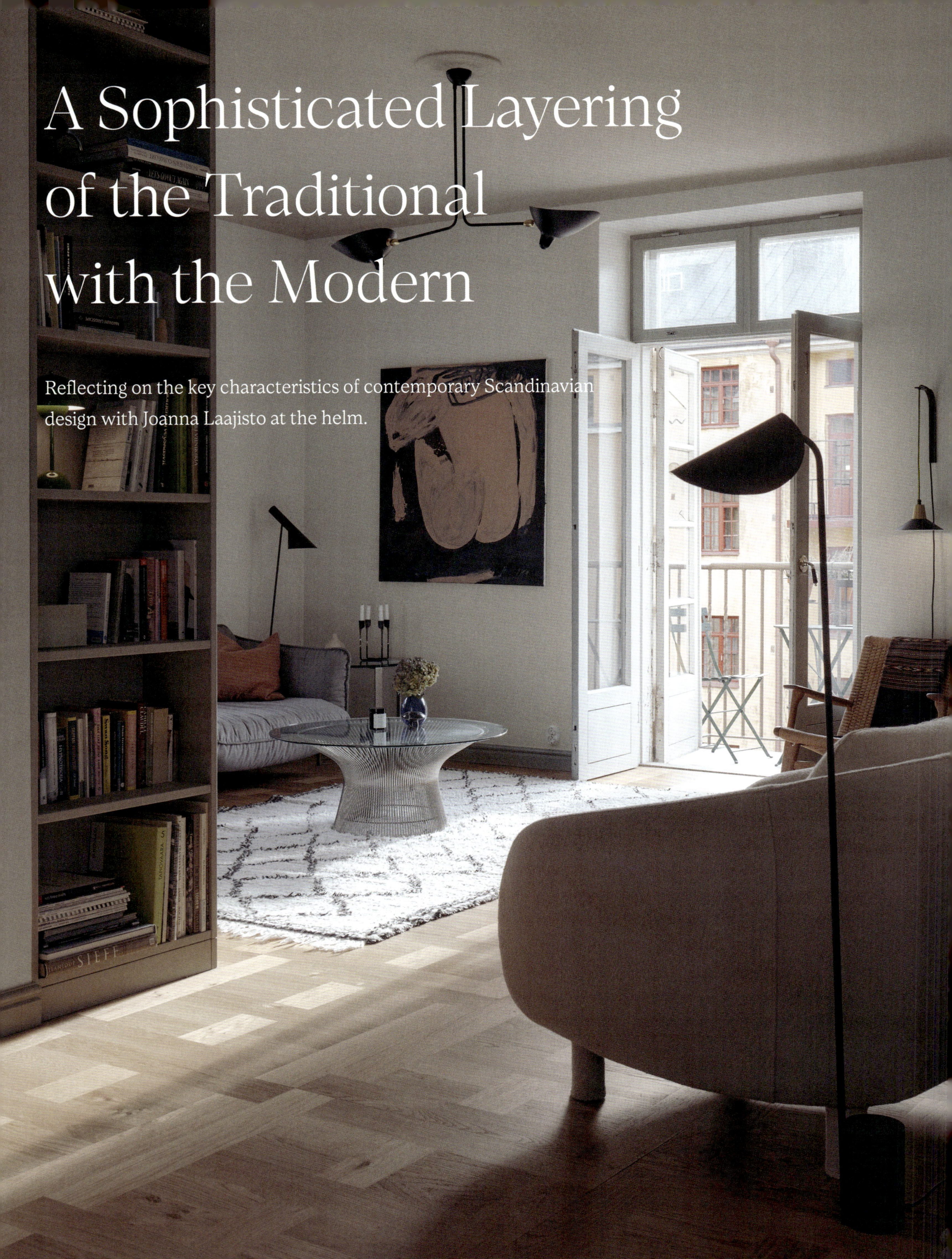

A Sophisticated Layering of the Traditional with the Modern

Reflecting on the key characteristics of contemporary Scandinavian design with Joanna Laajisto at the helm.

Opposite and above: Each room is minimally furnished and sees iconic midcentury pieces paired with contemporary models of Laajisto's own design.

HELSINKI APARTMENT
STUDIO JOANNA LAAJISTO
HELSINKI · FINLAND

Finnish interior architect and designer Joanna Laajisto is a champion of traditional Scandinavian style. She is also a devotee of modernism, acknowledging that the timeless classics of yesteryear never lose their appeal. In much of her work, she deftly demonstrates how the two can combine to create spaces of calm sophistication and class. The apartment Laajisto shares with her partner, photographer Mikko Ryhänen, and their children is a case in point.

Situated in an original 1920s apartment block in Helsinki, its rooms retain original molded skirting and architraves. Laajisto has paired them with a geometric parquet flooring of her own design. These elements, along with the paneled doors of the kitchen cabinets and a rustic tiled wall, lend a homely Scandinavian appeal. Yet they are layered with a carefully curated furniture selection that places contemporary Laajisto designs, such as the Bobo lounge chair and Lumme floor lamp, alongside midcentury classics—a Warren Platner coffee table, Bertoia's wire chairs, and Arne Jacobsen's AJ lamp—bringing a more elegant, urban edge to her design.

Opposite and above: A warm color palette of grays, creams, and the natural, honeyed browns of wood, wicker, and leather ties everything together.

Classic minimalist designs such as Arne Jacobsen's 1954 Dot Stool (opposite) and Joe Colombo's 1967 table lamp sit right at home in the sparsely furnished rooms.

New Spaces with Traditional Traces

In a small courtyard space in Stockholm, an old stable—neglected for decades—takes shape as a contemporary living space for a small family.

Opposite: Approaching the house from its equestrian path. Above: The pared-back kitchen / dining area, with Outline 02 chairs by Japanese designer Fumihito Ohashi.

Above: Much of the furniture in the house was custom-designed by Ateljé Nord's Henrik Sagen, including the dining table in the kitchen area and this three-legged stool.
Opposite: In the living room, with its solid sliding walnut-wood doors, a table—also designed by Henrik Sagen—has a stove insert and stands beside a three-seater Sofa N701 from Ethnicraft.

THE OLD STABLE

ATELJÉ NORD

STOCKHOLM, SWEDEN

What once served as a stable, long since consigned to garage and storage space, was given a fresh lease of life by Ateljé Nord when it was commissioned to repurpose the building as a family home. With its sleek, minimal lines and earthy palette, the new dwelling is characteristic of understated, contemporary Swedish design.

The exterior has a simple plaster facade and oak windows below a metal roof; inside, the floors are lined with limestone, soft and warm, beneath exposed-beam ceilings. From the entrance, accessed via an equestrian walkway into the courtyard, residents enter the living room and kitchen areas, while the more private rooms are toward the rear of the house. Not all is entirely "new," though. The building's original purpose finds expression throughout the interior design: the oak window shutters are reminiscent of old stable doors, and the walls are plastered in neutral tones; details such as doorknobs, rails, and the mixer taps in the kitchen and bathroom have a black metal finish in homage to traditional blacksmithing.

Opposite and above: The whole design is reminiscent of Japanese tradition—from the low-lying futon-style bed to the floor-to-ceiling, dark-wood carpentry with its strong vertical figuring, and from the skylights (five in total) that fill the rooms with a soft, diffuse light to the somber neutral palette.

Back to the Future: When Nordic and Scandinavian Design Conquered the World

How a healthy cross-pollination of design principles underpinned by the tenets of "less is more" and "funkis," or functionalism, spread from Nordic Europe to influence global trends for more than a century.

The first real international success of what we could call modern Nordic design took place at the Paris World's Fair of 1925, formally known as the "International Exhibition of Modern Decorative and Industrial Art." The exhibition by the Seine River greeted some 16 million visitors from April to October of that year. While best remembered as the high point for colorful jazz age Art Deco motifs, the more restrained and strict Nordic pavilions provided a breakthrough for the export of Scandinavian design. The Danish pavilion, designed by the architect Kay Fisker, showed one of the first chairs by a young Arne Jacobsen, while the Swedish pavilion won much praise for its decorative glassware from Orrefors. It also had a large model of the new Stockholm City Hall by Ragnar Östberg, a building completed to huge acclaim in 1923, helping to put Swedish architecture on the international map. The many overseas visitors to the exhibition helped pave the way for the export of Nordic design, with Orrefors glassworks finding new stockists abroad, including Heal's furniture store in London.

Opposite: Hans J. Wegner's iconic Shell Chair for Carl Hansen, designed in 1963, with its winglike seat and curved backrest.
Above: Aino and Alvar Aalto's home in Helsinki incorporated their workplace and a studio in which they showcased their designs.

Above: Hans Wegner's popular Wishbone Chair. Opposite: Also designed in 1949, by Nisse and Kajsa Strinning, the String modular system has become a staple of the Nordic interior.

This international interest in Nordic design and architecture was brought home in 1930 with the Stockholm Exhibition. Organized by Gregor Paulsson of the Swedish Society of Arts and Crafts, and with Gunnar Asplund as the chief architect, it was open for over four months and had some four million visitors at a time when the entire Swedish population was only six million people. While progressive and radical modernism was already present on the continent with architects such as Le Corbusier and Walter Gropius, as well as Alvar Aalto in Finland, the Stockholm Exhibition of 1930 marked the breakthrough of modernism in Sweden. The event also significantly influenced the direction of architecture and product design in the surrounding Nordic countries, with many Nordic architects and designers visiting the Stockholm Exhibition. Large windows, clean lines, and facades without decorations spoke of the future, while the furniture was made from shiny tubular steel, and the decorative items were made of black plastic resin and white molded glass. This coincided with the Social Democrats forming a Swedish government in 1932 on a welfare reform agenda. This Swedish form of modernism became a physical manifestation of the new ideological direction of a forward-looking country where modern ideas were combined with modern design. The Social Democrats would remain in power for the next 44 years (barring a three-month spell in 1936) and carry out large housing programs, and the rest of the Nordic countries soon took a similar path. Slightly softer in its look than the continental European form of modernism, this new Nordic architecture that arrived with the Stockholm Exhibition of 1930 was referred to as functionalism, which was soon shortened to "funkis."

A few years later, Finland was in focus when Alvar Aalto constructed a pavilion out of wood at the Paris World's Fair of 1937. He named it "Le bois est en marche," meaning "The wood is on the move." The Finnish pavilion was a radical departure from how national pavilions were expected to appear and certainly different from those of Germany, Italy, and the Soviet Union, then under the regimes of Hitler, Mussolini, and Stalin. It was here that Aalto first showed his now famous organically shaped glass vase, which was made at Karhula-Iittala glassworks in Finland. At first, it was referred to as the Paris glass, but after Alvar and Aino Aalto used the vases in the interiors of the luxurious Savoy restaurant in Helsinki, which was completed later the same year, it became known as the Savoy vase.

Alvar Aalto returned with a Finnish pavilion at the New York World's Fair of 1939, an event with some 44 million visitors, but was cut short by the outbreak of the Second World War. The architect Sven Markelius designed the Swedish pavilion. This was where the classic wooden Dala horse, the quintessential Swedish national symbol, was introduced to the United States; some seven thousand were sold, and a gigantic Dala horse was shipped across the Atlantic and placed outside the Swedish pavilion. One of the exhibitors inside the Swedish pavilion was Bruno Mathsson, a furniture designer and later architect who had also exhibited in Paris in 1937. There, his work was seen by Edgar Kaufmann Jr., who arranged for Mathsson's furniture to be used in the Museum of Modern Art in New York's Goodwin / Stone building, completed two years later. The museum also included Mathsson's furniture in several design exhibitions, the first in 1944, which exposed U.S. modernist architects who started including Mathsson's furniture in their interiors. Meanwhile, Alvar Aalto spent part of the war years in the United States, which culminated with his 1946–48 Baker House Dormitory for M.I.T. in Boston, USA. The U.S. critics were impressed by what they saw and found the Nordic form of modernism more humane and living-focused in form than that coming out of Germany, Switzerland, and France.

This U.S. interest in Nordic design and architecture laid the groundwork for a hugely influential touring exhibition in 1954, "Design in Scandinavia," the first major exhibition of Scandinavian design to travel to North America, and which also included works from Finland. The exhibition included over 700 objects and showcased ceramics, furniture, glassware, metalwork, and textiles from Denmark, Norway, Sweden, and Finland. It was pivotal in introducing modern Scandinavian design to North America and creating an interest from American stores and customers. It opened in New York's Brooklyn Museum in April 1954 and traveled throughout the United States and Canada until 1957. The show featured work by Alvar Aalto, Kay Bojesen, Kaj Franck, Finn Juhl, Henning Koppel, Timo Sarpaneva, Hans J. Wegner, and many others.

Equally important was the "H55 exhibition" in the town of Helsingborg in southern Sweden in the summer of 1955, overlooking the waters of Øresund and Helsingør in Denmark, a short ferry ride away. The theme was "Modern Man in the Environment." Recognized as a World's Fair, the design and architecture exhibition had exhibitors from Denmark, Sweden, Finland, Norway, the United Kingdom, West Germany, Japan, France, and Switzerland, but the focus was on Scandinavian design. Some of the most iconic and well-known design classics we still recognize today were shown here for the first time, including Kay Bojesen's wooden monkey, the 3107 chair by Arne Jacobsen, Astrid Sampe's Persons Kryddskåp textile print and the Terma series of oven ceramics by Stig Lindberg for Gustavsberg. Elissa Aalto, wife and partner of Alvar Aalto, created the iconic H55 pattern used in the Finnish pavilion, and many international visitors also saw the popular String shelving system by Swedish designers Kajsa and Nisse Strinning for the first time.

Among the most important international recognitions of Nordic design at this time were the awards given at the Milan Triennial. As the name says, this was an exhibition that took place every third year in Milan, Italy. During the 1950s, besides the Italian designers, it was dominated by medals awarded to the Nordic exhibitors, starting at the Milan Triennial IX in 1951 with a Gold Medal awarded to Danish textile designer Helga Foght and Finnish designers Timo Sarpaneva, Tapio Wirkkala, and Dora Jung, each winning a Grand Prix in 1954, while Arne Jacobsen won a Grand Prix in 1957 for a laminated chair that is now simply known as the Grand Prix chair. This exposure to designs from other parts of the world also led to a healthy cross-fertilization of ideas; U.S. West Coast midcentury design clearly has a Nordic influence, and so does British and Italian design of that time, but Nordic designers

were also bringing back new ideas. Danish designer Poul Kjærholm was clearly influenced by Mies van der Rohe in his furniture, while textile designers, like Finnish fabric designer Maija Isola, looked at British and American pop art.

It has been argued that it was the postwar export success of Scandinavian design that gave birth to flat-packed furniture; these bulky items were just too costly to send abroad otherwise. That might sound logical, but it was only the Thema dining chair by the Swedish designer Yngve Ekström from 1953 that first used the now classic six-sided hex key for self-assembly by the customers, sold flat-packed in a box. The Thema chair wasn't even intended for export but had been created as a budget line for the famous Stockholm department store Nordiska Kompaniet, which sold the chairs as a dining set under the laconic slogan "Four chairs in a box." Yngve Ekström later used hex keys and a knockdown design again for what has become his most famous furniture creation, the Lamino easy chair of 1956, which was celebrated for its comfort. When IKEA started to sell furniture in flat packs, the idea had been around in Sweden for a while already, ready to conquer the world.

During the 1960s and 1970s, the furniture fair in Copenhagen was of global importance, attracting buyers and journalists from around the world. This was the place to discover the latest interior design trends and products while admiring beautiful Copenhagen. During these Cold War decades, the progressive Nordic countries were seen as having the solutions to so many of the world's problems, offering a better form of society, and the furniture and interiors were an integral part of this. The most important publication was *Mobilia*, a magazine published from 1955 until 1984, with texts in English, German, and French, as well as Danish and Swedish. The demise of *Mobilia* coincided with a low point for Nordic design. Throughout the 1980s and 1990s, the most exciting products usually came from other places, Italy in particular, while the Nordics focused on public furniture and function but perhaps lacked verve.

In the 2000s, Sweden had a new wave of exciting designers, spearheaded by form givers like Thomas Sandell, Pia Wallén, Thomas Eriksson, and Jonas Bohlin. This made the Stockholm furniture fair one of the most exciting places on the global design circuit after Milan. Swedish designers like Claesson Koivisto Rune and Monica Förster were soon in demand by international manufacturers, not least many prestigious Italian brands, and continue to be so. The Danish design scene was also seeing a generational shift, and Danish brands like Hay, Muuto, Gubi, & Tradition, and Normann Copenhagen made up what became known as the "New Nordic" or "Danish Design 2.0," using Danish, Nordic, and global designers. With so many new brands, many new and exciting showrooms opened in the Danish capital. This has helped Copenhagen to return as the Nordic epicenter for interiors, not least with its "3 Days of Design" festival, which takes place in June each year. The most brilliant Danish design stars include Cecilie Manz, GamFratesi (Stine Gam and Enrico Fratesi), and Kasper Salto. Norway also has its share of modern designers, like Andreas Engesvik and Kristine Five Melvær or architect offices like Snøhetta. Over in Finland, there are Harri Koskinen, Ilkka Suppanen, and Klaus Haapaniemi. Finland also has a very long and important line of successful female designers, stretching back to the interiors of Aino Aalto in the 1930s, the textile designers at Marimekko from the 1950s onward to current designers like Nathalie Lahdenmäki, Johanna Gullichsen, and duo Mari Martikainen and Minna Impiö at Mifuko.

To see the best of this new Nordic design across its entire spectrum and to find out how to decorate a Nordic home like a native, a visit to each capital city is a must—whether it's homes, showrooms, public buildings, or design museums. The Nordic design and architecture scene is constantly evolving, driven by friendly competition across borders that spurs innovation. There is also an exchange of teachers and students across the many highly respected design and architecture universities in the Nordic countries. The Nordic home is never a fixed or given concept, and for that, we should be grateful.

Opposite: In recent times, furniture designs emerging under the New Nordic umbrella echo the timeless aesthetic of iconic midcentury pieces, as can be seen in Muuto's Midst pedestal table and shell-type Fiber Soft armchair.

A Timber-Clad Summer House on an Island of Its Own

Embracing the traditional building aesthetics of the region, this dwelling represents the epitome of rural Finnish living for modern times.

PROJECT Ö

ALEKSI HAUTAMÄKI AND MILLA SELKIMÄKI

ARCHIPELAGO NATIONAL PARK, FINLAND

Perched on the craggy tip of an island in Archipelago National Park, Finland, Project Ö is the creation of designers Aleksi Hautamäki and Milla Selkimäki and takes its name from the Swedish for "island" (Ö). Comprising two single-story volumes and reflecting the vernacular architecture, the buildings are long, low, and narrow, with vertical timber cladding beneath gabled roofs and large picture windows offering views in all directions. The island home is completely self-sufficient with solar panels on the roof and filtered seawater for drinking.

Inside, spaces are compact without compromising on functionality or comfort. The rooms are lined with wooden planks, and furnishings are minimal; kitchen cabinets are rendered in a matte-black finish. A key feature of each cabin is a covered outdoor space that sits at the mid-point so that the opposite ends can function separately. Ideally suited to long evenings on dreamy summer vacations, it means children can sleep in peace at one end while their parents socialize with friends at the other.

There is a space for alfresco dining between the two main volumes of the house.

Opposite: Since building the main dwelling, Aleksi Hautamäki and Milla Selkimäki have added a sauna, a workshop building, and a glass-lined dining pavilion.

Opposite and above: To be at one with nature, the couple built a sunken firepit close to the house and a dining deck and jetty on the waterfront.

The little granite and gneiss island is just one of more than 40,000 islands and islets in the Finnish Archipelago.

An Accomplished Vision of Nordic Modernism

This refined interpretation of Nordic Modernism showcases natural materials, white walls, a neutral palette, and functional, elegant furniture.

Opposite and above: On entering, visitors have views from the kitchen through the dining room to the living room, but also to the wild landscape beyond.

HOLIDAY HOME BY ÞINGVALLAVATN

KRADS

ÞINGVELLIR NATIONAL PARK, ICELAND

With vast picture windows that look out across a wild lakeside landscape, this dwelling in Þingvallavatn, Iceland, nestles into a densely overgrown hill, its black-timber-clad facades and gently sloping moss-covered roofs blending into the immediate surroundings. A vacation home for a pair of musicians, the house is the work of KRADS, an architectural studio based in Denmark and Iceland.

Free of the paraphernalia of day-to-day living, the home has spacious rooms that embrace the tenets of Nordic modernism to the max. Throughout, the floors are laid with Douglas fir, which, in a sunken seated area of the living room, rises to cover the room's end wall as well. Other walls and the ceilings are alternately painted white or lined with narrow timber slats, creating a constant play of light and texture. Almost all of the furniture is made from light wood in simple, geometric forms, from the island in the open-plan kitchen to the dining suite and various armchairs. In the living room, the sofas are upholstered in soft leather.

Opposite: The wooden staircase is veiled by a wall of timber louvers. Above, top: In the sunken living room, the rectangular tub can be covered and turned into a daybed.

A Contemporary Interior for a Rustic Retreat

Lying deep in Swedish woodland, this forest retreat sees the refurbishment of a traditional cabin to form a two-story house with a guest annex.

Above: The architects enlarged the windows, using them to frame different valley and forest views, but also to allow more natural daylight into the home.

Above: Though sparsely furnished, materials have been chosen throughout for their inherent warmth and texture, ensuring that spaces never feel empty or bleak.

FOREST RETREAT

NORM ARCHITECTS

SWEDEN

The work of Norm Architects, a Danish firm that prides itself on its minimalist interiors, the retreat is equipped simply with the bare essentials for slow living. The key to the success of this design lies in the delicate balance between the contemporary and the rustic to create an impression of space while ensuring a feeling of warmth and comfort.

Slender floor-to-ceiling doors stretch the height of the dwelling visually, making rooms feel taller. The architects used Dolomite plaster for the walls, which renders a soft, lightly textured surface. Worked in a pale gray and paired with oak timber flooring, it provides the ideal backdrop for the combination rustic and contemporary furnishings. There is a strong emphasis on natural materials, from the rough-hewn wooden pedestals, stone vessels, and rustic basketware to exquisitely crafted kitchen cabinetry and elegant furniture, among them pieces designed by the architects themselves. The palette is resolutely neutral throughout.

Above: The bed in this room runs parallel to a large window framing a forest view, so that on waking, the inhabitant feels totally immersed in the natural environment.

Material Honesty for Low-Tech Living

What was once an old fisherman's cottage among the sand dunes is now a contemporary guesthouse for wave-hunters and enthusiasts of slow living.

Opposite and above: With big skies above the low-lying sand dunes, natural daylight floods into the house through huge picture windows on all sides.

Above: Two of the home's three double bedrooms include storage with an integrated custom-made bunk bed for extra sleeping space.
Opposite: Looking straight through the living room, with its floor-to-ceiling picture windows. Tones both inside and outside the house are carefully matched.

VIPP COLD HAWAII

HAHN LAVSEN AND JULIE CLOOS MØLSGAARD

THY NATIONAL PARK, DENMARK

Nestled among the sand dunes of Denmark's largest national park, on a stretch of surf-worthy coastline dubbed "Cold Hawaii," this guesthouse embraces bold minimalism in a design centered on just five materials: aerated concrete, wood, stainless steel, glass, and brick. Whitewashed inside and out, the walls are built from insulated aerated concrete blocks beneath an untreated Douglas fir roof.

Inside, rooms lined with exposed brick floors are furnished with eclectic pieces that range from a custom-made, oak-fronted, modular kitchen by Vipp to more rustic finds from neighboring craft shops and work by local artists. A built-in custom fireplace in bush-hammered stone is mirrored on both sides of the gable that defines the living and dining areas. Colors are predominantly warm and sandy, with tones and textures inspired by the surrounding beaches, dunes, and cliffs, while natural woven fibers add a tailored textured layer. Spaces are calm and comfortable, allowing guests to unwind surrounded by untamed nature.

Cold Hawaii. With wind conditions akin to those of Hawaii, but freezing water, this stretch of Danish coastline has fostered a new Nordic extreme surf culture.

Opposite: There is a sense of calm inside the house—a deliberate counter to the wildness of the terrain beyond the windows.
Above: Maintaining the same textures and colorways throughout the house—in the wood, the brickwork, and textiles—ensures harmony throughout.

Opposite and above: The house nestles in the sandy dunes. Lush with vegetation, the dunes are green through summer, turning to a warm, amber glow as fall leads into winter.

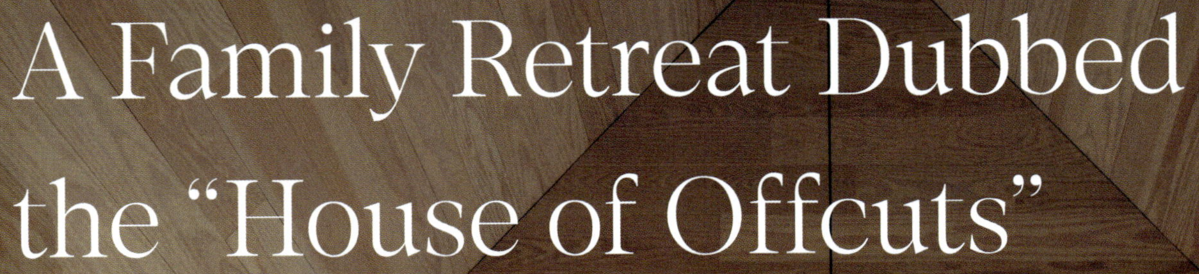

A Family Retreat Dubbed the "House of Offcuts"

In a reassessment of historical building vocabularies, the architects clad an oak-timber-framed house in offcuts from Danish firm Dinesen's traditional wooden floors.

Above: The architects built the house around the existing terrain, negotiating rocks, plants, and trees rather than attempting to reshape the landscape.

SALTVIGA HOUSE

KOLMAN BOYE ARCHITECTS

LILLESAND, NORWAY

In Saltviga House, Kolman Boye Architects explore the idea of using offcuts from Dinesen wood floors to make shingle-like panels for external cladding. It is a move that serves to ennoble the scrap material while offering a credible approach to building homes more sustainably.

The house sits on a bluff, facing the sea of Skagerrak in southeastern Norway, where the oak offcuts blend in beautifully with the landscape of granite, lichen, and conifers. Following the lie of the land, the house is set on five levels and divided into two main volumes—one housing communal spaces and the other for more private rooms. A central hallway offers views across the house and toward a wall of glass overlooking the sea. In contrast to the rustic-looking exterior, interior rooms are lined with light-colored planks of Douglas fir and paired with warm, polished concrete used for floors and work surfaces in the kitchen and a central fireplace in the living room. Furnishings combine vintage and contemporary Scandinavian designs.

Opposite: Each space inside the house has a distinct volume and ceiling height. Dcuglas fir-lined walls and ceilings balance beautifully with the neutral screed floors.

Opposite: The exterior oak cladding will turn silvery-gray over time to blend in seamlessly with the slate and granite landscape.

Lofty, Timber-Lined Spaces beneath a Thatched Roof

Located in Skagen, the northernmost point in Denmark, this summer house pays tribute to local architecture and the history of the town.

SKAGEN KLITGÅRD
PAX ARCHITECTS
SKAGEN, DENMARK

The design of the house, with its blackened timber facades and thatched roof, draws inspiration from the region's Black Period—a time when charred wood from shipwrecks was a primary construction material and roofs were covered in straw.

Serving as a summerhouse to be used by three generations of the same family, the dwelling features a series of fluid zones in which freestanding elements, such as the fireplace, create smaller spaces so that the central kitchen, suitable for get-togethers, is surrounded by more intimate spaces for solitary activities. No matter where you are in the house, however, the pitched roof above remains continuous, reinforcing a feeling of "being under one roof." Windows with thick oak frames feature on both sides of the house, blurring the lines between the interior and the exterior. A primary material, Douglas fir, is used for everything, from the exposed beams to the light-colored floors and the finely crafted cabinetry in the kitchen. Dominant colors are muted, reflecting those of the surroundings.

The black facades and deep, thatched roof have become part of the Skagen landscape, which is rough and harsh, yet beautiful.

Opposite: A central theme of the design was to offer uninterrupted views along the long facades of the house, to both bind the house together, but also to its surroundings.

Opposite and above: Views through the house, from the dining room to the living room and toward the kitchen. The sunlight makes wonderful contrasts in the space.

Above: The kitchen area opens out onto the terraced space outside, which is the primary gathering place for family members during the summer season.

The thatched roof is in close dialogue with the local vegetation, while the gap between wall and roof gives the architecture a certain airiness.

A Celebration of Finnish Art, Architecture, and Artistry

The home, studio, and gallery space of celebrated ceramicist Karin Widnäs is a triumph of contemporary Finnish design.

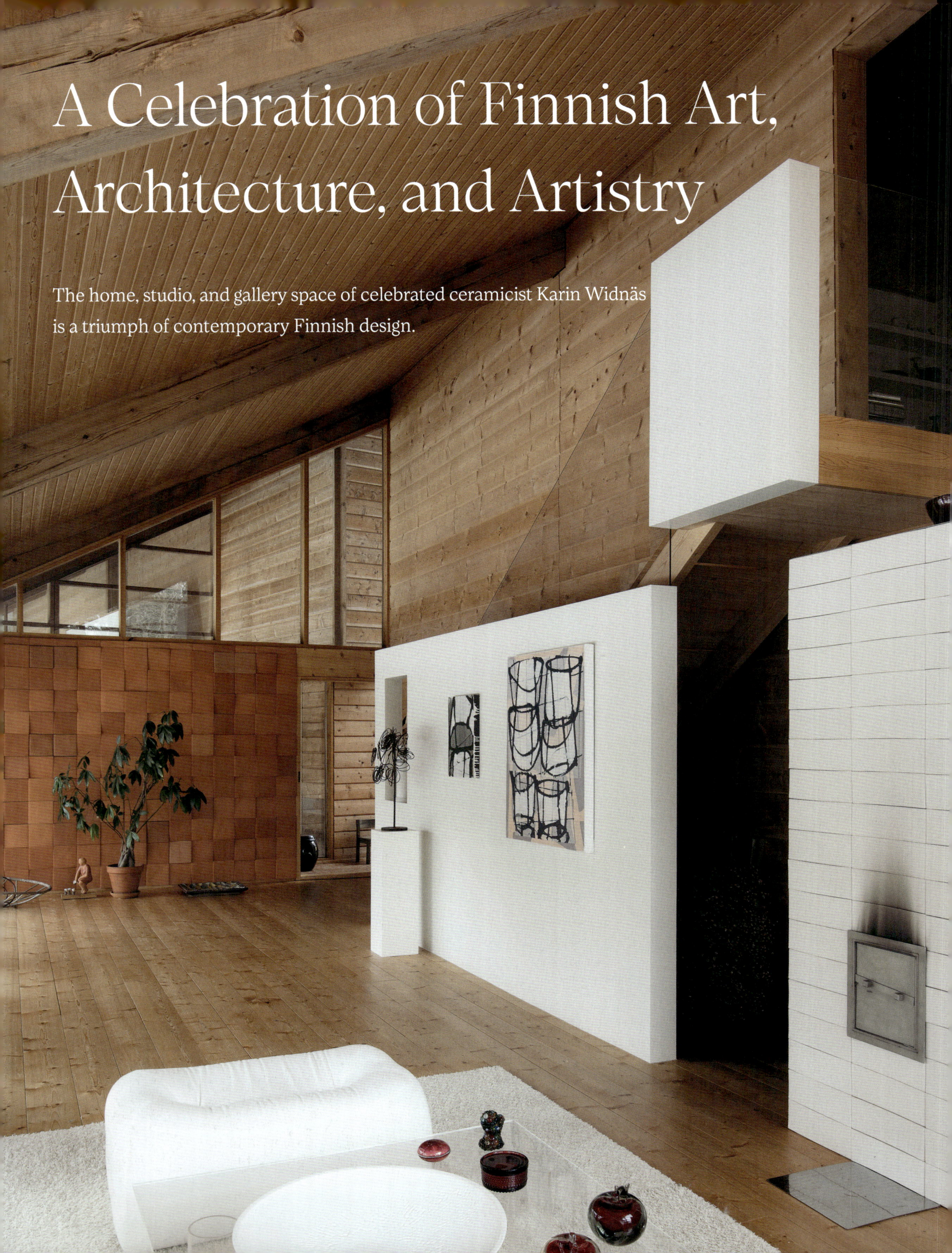

Opposite and above: Predominantly wooden with black and white decor, the building is a sanctuary of architecture, light, aesthetic interiors, and ceramic art.

Above: A steep, pitched roof and walls made of glass panels allow for maximum natural daylight to fill the lofty spaces.
Opposite, top: Clad in blackened wood, the house has a timeworn appearance and blends in seamlessly with the wooded Finnish landscape.

STUDIO KARIN WIDNÄS
TUOMO SIITONEN ARCHITECTS
FISKARS, FINLAND

In the village of Fiskars, in southern Finland, lies the striking atelier home of ceramicist Karin Widnäs. The design was a collaboration between the artist and Helsinki-based architect Professor Tuomo Siitonen. Widnäs's fascination with merging her ceramic finishes with architecture was key to its creation. The result is a two-story timber structure in which walls and floors are lined with terra-cotta tiles, handmade using traditional Finnish techniques.

Sunlight floods through floor-to-ceiling windows, creating an artful display of light and shadow across their earthy surfaces. The house has a streamlined interior with doors, windows, a staircase, and paneled hallway crafted by local cabinetmakers. Minimal furnishings, predominantly in white, make for the perfect space to showcase the artist's extensive collection of ceramic art from the 1960s to the present day. Among many standout pieces are a large vessel by Erna Aaltonen and a ceramic bowl by Riitta Talonpoika—both artists in the local community.

Opposite and above: The living room is sparsely furnished with modern white furniture and artwork made by friends of the ceramicist.

Opposite: A covered outdoor area between the artist's home and studio. In stark contrast to the interior, exterior spaces are dark and enveloping.
Above, top left: The complex structure of the roof creates a deep overhang, which offers shelter for a timber walkway that surrounds the entire house.

A Masterclass in Danish Interior Design

Blending form and function with the utmost harmony, furniture designer Børge Mogensen's house is a triumph of midcentury design.

Above: The house stands in a lush neighborhood that, at the time, was known as "the architects' marsh" due to the number of designers who chose to build houses there.

BØRGE MOGENSEN'S HOME

BØRGE MOGENSEN, ARNE KARLSEN, AND ERLING ZEUTHEN NIELSEN

GENTOFTE, DENMARK

The floor-to-ceiling windows of Børge Mogensen's house, which was completed in 1958, fill the interior with a soft light, and each room sees natural materials in earthy colors working together to create warm, welcoming, tranquil spaces. In rooms overlooking the garden, geometric brick paving matches that of the yard outside, and the walls and vaulted ceiling are lined with dark timbers. At the heart of the house, the living room is a generous open space with light-hued timber floors and weathered, whitewashed brick walls.

The house is furnished throughout with Mogensen's designs—elegant yet unpretentious pieces carefully crafted to balance comfort and durability. In the living room, the 2213 leather-upholstered sofa designed specifically for the space faces two Spanish Chairs made from oak and leather with broad armrests. The ever-practical, extendable oak BM71 Library Table stands in the study. And in the garden room, beside a compact set of BM375 Nesting Tables, awaits the iconic Hunting Chair—angular, low-slung, and inviting.

Opposite: In the dining room stands Mogensen's 6386 Dining Table and a set of his J39 Chairs with hand-woven seats. Above: His iconic Club 2213 three-seat leather sofa.

Opposite and this page, top right: One of Mogensen's best-known designs, the Spanish Chair, was inspired by traditional styles the designer had seen on his travels in Spain.

Above: Mogensen's study, affectionately dubbed the "laboratory." It was in this space that many of his furniture designs originated.

A Cottage That Seems to Grow from the Landscape

This cozy refuge perches precariously on granite bedrock, its two levels adapting to the uneven terrain of a Norwegian archipelago.

VEGA COTTAGE
KOLMAN BOYE ARCHITECTS
VEGA, NORWAY

Taking its cues from the traditional sheds, cabins, and boathouses of the region, this timber-clad cottage stands on the island of Vega in the Vegaøyan archipelago and takes shape as two pitch-roofed volumes slightly offset from one another. Not far from the Arctic Circle, this is a remote, rugged spot, and from within the cottage, large picture windows look out in three directions to frame views of the Norwegian Sea, the mountains, and the gnarled-birch-strewn bedrock, respectively.

The cottage has a compact plan with generous communal spaces on the lower level and smaller-scale bedrooms upstairs. Midcentury-style furnishings populate the living and dining areas, the spaces arranged around a central stone hearth. The walls are finished in linseed-oil-painted pine with untreated birch skirting and window frames. Decoration is kept to the absolute minimum, allowing for the natural materials to speak for themselves in an interior that feels as pristine as the landscape it inhabits.

The inhabitants of this timber-clad cottage are completely surrounded by the rough and rugged terrain of the Vegaøyan archipelago.

Opposite: The living room, prior to furnishing. It has a gallery-like ambience, its large windows set within pristine, whitewashed walls and a ceiling.

Opposite and above: The house is simply furnished throughout, with predominantly wooden furniture and textiles in earthy browns, creams, and grays.

Blending Nordic Sensibility with a Japanese Aesthetic

Natural materials in the colors of the local coastal landscape dominate a design that seamlessly mixes Nordic coziness with Japanese traditions.

Above: The dwelling consists of four interconnected wooden structures nestled into the rock face and surrounded by a spacious deck offering stunning views.

Above: A double-height living area is divided by an industrial kitchen island (left), offering both lounge (right) and dining spaces with panoramic views.

ARCHIPELAGO HOUSE

NORM ARCHITECTS

SWEDEN

Taking inspiration from local boathouse building traditions, this Swedish coastal summerhouse blends harmoniously with the surrounding landscape inside and out. Clad in timber that is beginning to silver, the dwelling is set into a cliff and is arranged on five levels that follow the natural slope of the terrain.

Inside, the styling combines Nordic coziness with a Japanese aesthetic to create generous, open-plan spaces furnished with high-quality contemporary pieces. There is a focus on natural materials that include wood, stone, soft textiles, and marble, and the color palette has been carefully chosen to reflect the rugged terrain outside—taupes, creams, grays, and greens. The rooms feature furnishings designed by the architects, some of which take inspiration from Japanese tradition, such as the marble-topped coffee table, the cone-shaped paper pendant lamps, and stoneware in monochrome tones. Meanwhile, most of the seating furniture embodies a more typical Scandinavian sensibility.

Opposite: In the dining room, the large table is surrounded by a set of dining chairs beneath a washi paper pendant light, all designed by the architects. This page: The Japanese aesthetic is evident in pleasing geometry of the styling throughout and the black ceramic vessels lining the kitchen shelves.

Above: Created specifically for this interior, the N-CC01 round-backed chair was designed by Norm Architects and made in collaboration with Japan-based manufacturers Karimoku Case.

A Site-Specific Summerhouse on the Gothenburg Archipelago

Imitating the characteristics of its rocky surroundings, this house appears as a collection of individual, shifting volumes.

Previous pages and above: Each of the home's four volumes have a different function. The first is for sleeping and bathing, the second for cooking and dining, the third houses the living room, and the fourth, smaller volume is a tool shed.

VILLA VASSDAL
MNMT ARCHITECTURE
GOTHENBURG, SWEDEN

Situated on a small island in the Gothenburg archipelago, Sweden, Villa Vassdal takes shape as a low-lying cluster of buildings whose forms mimic the scale and rise and fall of the rocks among which they nestle. The entire structure is clad in untreated heart pine, which will gradually take on the mottled, grayish hues of the surrounding landscape.

Inside, the arrangement of the volumes defines the layout of the house, each marking a shift in function, while the ceilings follow the pitch of the roofs in a zigzag pattern. The main living spaces are oriented toward the sea, where large sliding doors open onto an external deck. And as the exterior is finished in wood so, too, is the interior. The walls and ceilings are lined with birch plywood, and there is solid timber underfoot. Internal doors, shelving, and most of the furniture are primarily wooden—contemporary in style and accompanied by soft furnishings in warm orange, blue, green, and yellow tones.

The orientation of the interior spaces is such that inhabitants are shielded from ne ghbors and harsh sunlight, but can enjoy uninterrupted views out to sea.

Though the living area (opposite) and the kitchen (above) are at opposite ends of the same open-plan space, each has a different relationship to the exterior.

A Modern Take on the Traditional Finnish Log House

In the hands of interior designer Laura Seppänen, this family home features classic and contemporary Danish furnishings set against flawless spruce wood surfaces.

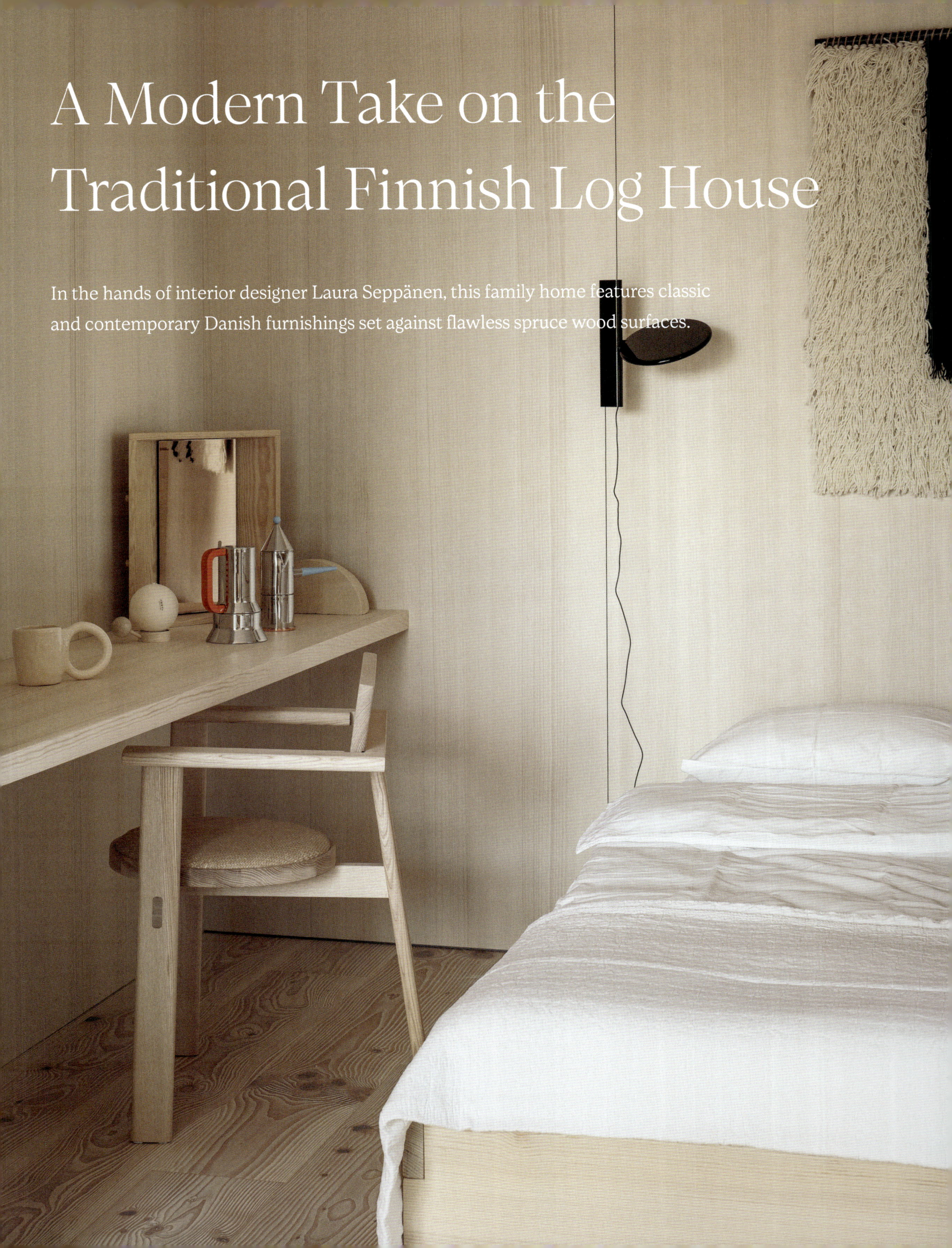

Opposite and above: The design does not just feature light-colored timber walls and floors, but has many light wooden furnishings and ornaments, too.

Above: Rounded shapes in rugs and curved furniture, such as the kitchen counter, add softness to this otherwise angular house.
Opposite: In the living room, besides Laura Seppänen's Lollipop chair and Arc rug, are an Epic coffee table from Gubi and an Interface Toastie modular sofa.

VILLA HAVU

LAURA SEPPÄNEN AND SANKARI ARCHITECTS

LOVIISA, FINLAND

Villa Havu is a modern log house designed by Jarkko Niiranen of Helsinki-based Sankari Architects in Loviisa, Finland, a coastal town on the craggy Gulf of Finland. Covering almost 2,000 square feet (185 square meters), the dwelling, in fact, comprises three buildings—the main single-story house, a small atelier, and a separate sauna.

Interior designer Laura Seppänen's vision was to line almost all surfaces with light-colored spruce wood, color-matching the timbers as closely as possible throughout. The resulting spaces are sleek and contemporary, yet they also exude a warmth and coziness that will grow richer as the wood ages. To complement the wood, Seppänen furnished the house with predominantly Finnish pieces, including a custom-made kitchen by Saari-keittiöt and stone bathroom units and fixtures crafted by Louhi Stones. When it comes to the furniture, pieces designed by Seppänen herself—including a striped Lollipop chair and the round high-tufted Arc rug in the living room—sit alongside Finnish classics, such as Alvar Aalto's 611 dining chairs.

Opposite: Looking toward the kitchen from the living room. Among the furniture here are the slender Radice bar stools from Mattiazzi and the more chunky AA Bench from Vaarnii. This page: Matching the spruce wood in all rooms of the house—from sauna to bedrooms and living spaces—guarantees that all surfaces will age at the same pace.

A guest bedroom (opposite) and a living room (above). The same limited palette of black, white, gray, and natural wood runs throughout the entire development.

Index

MNMT Architecture
formerly Studio Holmberg
mnmt.se

VILLA VASSDAL
Gothenburg, Sweden
Photography: Markus Bülow, markusbulow.com
pp. 238 – 245

Børge Mogensen, Arne Karlsen, and Erling Zeuthen Nielsen

BØRGE MOGENSEN'S HOME
Gentofte, Denmark
Photography courtesy of Fredericia, fredericia.com
pp. 216 – 223

Nichetto Studio
nichettostudio.com

PINK VILLA
Stockholm, Sweden
Photography courtesy of Nichetto Studio
pp. 80 – 85

Norm Architects
normcph.com

FOREST RETREAT
Sweden
Photography: Jonas Bjerre-Poulsen, jonasbjerrepoulsen.com
pp. 174 – 179

ARCHIPELAGO HOUSE
Sweden
Photography: Jonas Bjerre-Poulsen, jonasbjerrepoulsen.com
pp. 230 – 237

Vuokko and Antti Nurmesniemi

VUOKKO AND ANTTI NURMESNIEMI HOUSE
Helsinki, Finland
Photography: ASUN / Studio Koskinen Rantanen, asun.fi
Sameli Rantanen
pp. 94, 96 – 99;
Pyry Rantanen
p. 95

PAX Architects
pax.dk

HILL HOUSE
Helgenæs, Denmark
Photography: Ida Schmidt, idaschmidt.photography
pp. 40 – 43, 45 – 48
Thomas Bossel
p. 44

BOULDER HOUSE
Østbirk, Denmark
Photography courtesy of PAX architects
pp. 126 – 129

SKAGEN KLITGÅRD
Skagen, Denmark
Photography: Rasmus Hjortshøj, rasmushjortshoj.com
pp. 198 – 207

Sanden+Hodnekvam Architects
sandenhodnekvam.no

HOUSE ON PILLARS
Nesodden, Norway
Photography: Thomas Ekstrøm, thomasekstrom.com
pp. 8, 49, 50, 51 top left, bottom right / left, 52 / 53
Courtesy of Sanden+Hodnekvam Architects
pp. 48, 51 top right

Laura Seppänen LS Design Agency
lauraseppanen.com

VILLA HAVU
Loviisa, Finland
Achitectural Design: Jarkko Niiranen / Sankari Arkkitehdit
Interior Design: Laura Seppänen / LS Design Agency
Photography: Mikael Pettersson
pp. 246 – 253

Louise Skafte and Johannes Lauridsen
@johanneslauridsen

SJÆLLANDS ODDE HOME
Sjællands Odde, Denmark
Styling: Rikke Graff Juel
Photography: Christina Kayser O. / Living Inside, livinginside.it
pp. 24 – 31

Emily and Christian Soneson

SUMMER HIDEAWAY
Dalarö, Sweden
Photography: Jonas Ingerstedt, ingerstedt.se
pp. 32 – 39

Studio Joanna Laajisto
joannalaajisto.com

HELSINKI APARTMENT
Helsinki, Finland
Photography: Mikko Ryhänen, mikkoryhanen.com
pp. 6 left, 142 – 147
Serge Mouille, Pendant Lamp
© VG Bild-Kunst, Bonn 2024
p. 142

Johan Sundberg Arkitektur
johansundberg.com

SOMMARHOUSE SOLVIKEN
Mölle, Sweden
Associate Architect: Itziar del Río Gómiz
Photography courtesy of Johan Sundberg Arkitektur / Peo Olsson, peoolsson.se
pp. 122 – 125

SUMMERHOUSE H
Lilla Beddinge, Sweden
Associate Architects: Itziar del Río Gómiz and Henrik Ålund
Photography courtesy of Johan Sundberg Arkitektur / Markus Linderoth, @markuslinderoth
pp. 130 – 135

Tuomo Siitonen Architects
tsi.fi

STUDIO KARIN WIDNÄS
Fiskars, Finland
Photography: Niclas Mäkelä, niclasmakela.com
pp. 208 – 215

Vipp
vipp.com

VIPP COLD HAWAII
Thy National Park, Denmark
Kitchen, Furniture, and Lighting: Vipp
Architect: Hahn Lavsen
Interior Design: Julie Cloos Mølsgaard
Photography: Pia Winther, piawinther.dk
pp. 180 – 189

Additional Credits

Taina Sohlman / Alamy Stock Photo (p. 104);
Brian Ormerod Photographer / Alamy Stock Photo (p. 105);
Yegorovnick / Alamy Stock Photo (p. 106);
HelloWorld Images / Alamy Stock Photo (p. 107);
FP Collection / Alamy Stock Photo (p. 108);
Juniors Bildarchiv GmbH / Alamy Stock Photo (p. 109);
Nick Harrison / Alamy Stock Photo (p. 155)
Classic Picture Library / Alamy Stock Photo (p. 157)
Courtesy of Muuto, muuto.com (p. 158)

The Nordic Home

Scandinavian Living, Interiors, and Design

This book was conceived, edited, and designed by gestalten.

Edited by *Robert Klanten* and *Masha Erman*

Editorial support by *Effie Efthymiadi* and *Laura Allsop*

Introduction and features by *Magnus Englund*
Project texts and captions by *Anna Southgate*

Editorial Management: *Arndt Jasper*
Photo Editor: *Zoe Paterniani*

Design, layout, and cover by *Joana Sobral*
Typeface: Loretta by *Abel Martins* and *Joana Correia*

Cover image: Børge Mogensen, Arne Karlsen, and Erling Zeuthen Nielsen, Børge Mogensen Home, Photography courtesy of Fredericia, fredericia.com
Backcover image: Kolman Boye Architects, Saltviga House, Photography by Johan Dehlin, johandehlinphotography.com

Printed by DZS Grafik, Ljubljana, Slovenia
Made in Europe

Published by gestalten, Berlin 2024
ISBN 978-3-96704-168-2

For more information, and to order books, please visit www.gestalten.com

Bibliographic information published by the Deutsche Nationalbibliothek.
The Deutsche Nationalbibliothek lists this publication in the Deutsche Nationalbibliografie; detailed bibliographic data is available online at www.dnb.de

None of the content in this book was published in exchange for payment by commercial parties or designers; the inclusion of all work is based solely on its artistic merit.

This book was printed on paper certified according to the standards of the FSC®.